Book Three

Monster Problems

By

R.L. Ullman

Monster Problems 3

Copyright © 2020 by R.L. Ullman.

All rights reserved. This book or any portion thereof may not be reproduced or used in any manner whatsoever without the express written permission of the publisher except for the use of brief quotations in a book review.

Cover design by Yusup Mediyan
All character images created with heromachine.com.

Published by But That's Another Story... Press
Ridgefield, CT

Printed in the United States of America.

First Printing, 2020.

ISBN: 978-1-7340612-5-3
Library of Congress Control Number: 2020908132

To Lou and Henry,
thanks for keeping an eye on things

Growing up in a superhero family is cool, unless you're powerless.

Don't miss the bestselling, award-winning series by R.L. Ullman

EPIC ACTION! EPIC LAUGHS! EPIC FUN!

TABLE OF CONTENTS

1.	Blood Hunt	1
2.	School Daze	13
3.	Monsters Unleashed	24
4.	Give Me the Dirt	35
5.	Agent M	45
6.	The Great Escape	55
7.	Monsters on the Run	68
8.	An Unexpected Guest	77
9.	Too Little Too Late	90
10.	Bad Blood	101
11.	Raising the Stakes	110
12.	Relatively Speaking	121
13.	Almost There	133
14.	Double Cross	144
15.	The Last at Bat	153
Epilogue	The Aftermath	164

CHAPTER ONE

BLOOD HUNT

I'm in bat-form, soaring high above the city.

It's well after midnight and a full moon hangs in the night sky. I don't remember how I got here, but the cool air feels good against my skin. It's peaceful among the clouds and I spread my wings, riding the air currents to a higher altitude.

From my vantage point, the city below looks abandoned, absent of any signs of life. Other than the streetlamps lining the roads, there isn't a light to be found inside the many homes and apartments. Yet, despite how empty the city looks, I know it's filled with people.

Sleeping people.

And I'm ravenously hungry.

My stomach rumbles and churns like I haven't eaten for days. Of course, I know that isn't true, but despite what my head is telling me, the longing in my stomach is only growing stronger.

It feels like a craving.

A craving I must satisfy.

One

With each flap of my wings, I feel my strength slipping away. If I don't feed soon I'll lose energy. I pulse my radar across the sprawling, concrete landscape, looking for my best opportunity. Finding an open window would make things a whole lot easier, and there are literally hundreds of windows to choose from.

But which one should I pick?

Then, I spot it.

There's a three-story brownstone with a brick stairway out front. For some reason, this particular building is calling to me, but I don't know why. I scan the windows which are shut except for one on the third floor.

I zero in and land on the windowsill.

The room inside is pitch black, but that's not an issue for me. As I look around the tiny room, I notice the minimal accommodations. There's a bed, a dresser, a desk, and little else. Not that it matters, because I'm not here for the décor, but rather for what's lying in the bed.

As I stare at the figure snuggled in the blankets, I suddenly feel an overwhelming sense of guilt. I mean, this is crazy. Am I really going to do this?

Am I really going to suck someone's blood?

Suddenly, I have a change of heart. I back up to fly away when my stomach grumbles again. Ugh. I'm so hungry and regular food just won't satisfy my craving.

Maybe I'll move a little closer.

I hop off the windowsill onto the cold floor and concentrate on becoming a kid again. Seconds later, I'm back in human-form standing over a curly-haired boy who looks about my age. His head is resting on his pillow and he's snoring lightly, the nape of his neck exposed.

I lick my lips and lean forward.

And then I stop myself.

I mean, I've never actually done this before. But I won't take a lot of blood, just enough to get rid of this crazy hunger. And if I'm gentle enough maybe he won't even wake up. Then, I'll fly out of here and he'll never know the difference.

It seems easy enough.

But suddenly, I feel a wave of disgust. What am I doing? The last time I checked, I wasn't a full-fledged vampire. But if that's true, what am I doing here?

I think back to my conversation with Dr. Renfield at the Van Helsing Academy. He said it was only a matter of time before my father's vampire genes took over my mother's human genes. And once that happens, the molecular structure of my body will become less Natural and more Supernatural, impacting my thoughts and behaviors.

In other words, I'll be a true vampire.

Is that why I'm here?

Has it already happened?

I've got to get out of here!

I take a step back and land on something round! My foot rolls and I SMACK hard into the wall behind me. Fortunately, I manage to grab the windowsill before

One

toppling over.

Great job, Bram. Could I be any clumsier? And when I look down I see a baseball lying next to my foot.

Awesome. I just hope I didn't wake—

"Hey!" the boy says, sitting up. "Who are you?"

"Um, no one," I say, getting back to my feet. "You're just having a dream. Don't worry, I'll be going now."

"Bram?" the boy says. "Is that you?"

Bram?

How'd he know my name?

But as I look closer at his face, my jaw drops, because I can't believe my eyes. That curly hair! It's Johnny! My orphan friend!

But how?

Now I know why everything seems so familiar. Without even realizing it, I flew back to the New England Home for Troubled Boys! And I was about to drink Johnny's blood!

Suddenly, I feel sick to my stomach.

"Bram?" he says, looking closer. "It is you! I'd recognize those ears anywhere. What are you doing here?" Then, his eyes go wide as he grabs his throat. "Were you trying to hurt me?"

"N-No," I stammer.

"I-I don't believe you," he says. "You came through my window! You were going to suck my blood!"

"No!" I insist.

"Br—"

***

"—am?"

"No!" I yell, sitting up, sweat pouring from my forehead.

"Bram?" Rage repeats, staring down at me with a puzzled look on his face. "Um, are you okay?"

"What?" I say, looking around. Where am I? What happened to Johnny?

Then, I realize I'm lying in my bed at the Van Helsing Academy.

I glance at our shut window and realize it was all a dream. I was never at the New England Home for Troubled Boys. I never tried to drink Johnny's blood. I flop down on my pillow relieved.

"Are you okay?" Rage asks. "You look kind of pale, even for you."

"Yeah," I say, catching my breath. "I'm good. Just had a really bad dream."

"Should I get Van Helsing?" Rage asks. "The last time you had a really bad dream you kind of endangered the whole school, remember?"

Van Helsing?

"Oh, no," I say quickly. "It wasn't anything like that. I'm good. Really."

I try looking calm, but I'm totally freaked out right now. And truthfully, Van Helsing is the last person I want

One

to share my dream with because I'm not exactly sure I can trust him.

When I fought Count Dracula at Dr. Moreau's tower, he opened my eyes to Van Helsing. Now, I know Count Dracula isn't the most reliable source of information, but he said a few things that rang true. He reminded me that Van Helsing descends from generations of vampire hunters who dedicated their lives to the complete extermination of all vampires. And since only a vampire can kill another vampire, Count Dracula said Van Helsing is just using me to get rid of him.

And then, I'll be next.

I don't want to believe him, but Van Helsing has withheld things from me before. And strangely, it was Count Dracula who gave me tips on how to use my powers better. But that wasn't all Count Dracula had to offer.

He asked me to join him.

He said I am what I am for a reason. He said I could try fighting my destiny but it wouldn't work because my vampire tendencies will slowly take over my soul.

I tried to ignore him, but based on my dream, I'm afraid he might be right. And I'm scared.

"Big day today," Rage says, grabbing his backpack from his bed. "Are you ready?"

"Ready?" I say. "Ready for what?"

"For end of term exams," Rage says, looking at me like I'm nuts. "You know, the thing we've been studying like crazy for over the last few weeks? On second thought, maybe I should get Van Helsing to look at you."

End of term exams? That's right!

I rub my eyes and exhale. Right now, the last thing I want to do is take exams.

"No, I'm good," I say, swinging my legs out of bed. "They just slipped my mind for a second. Wishful thinking, I guess."

"I guess," Rage says. "Well, just to remind you, our exams are today. And in case you also forgot, you have to pass them to move on with our section."

"I know, I know," I say, standing up and stretching. "I'm not planning on failing. But I am worried about InvisiBill. You think he knows his stuff?"

"He'd better," Rage says. "Aura's been grilling him non-stop for days. If he fails he'll not only have to repeat the coursework, but he'll have to answer to her too."

"Then he'd better pass," I say.

Just then, my stomach rumbles.

"I think you need breakfast," Rage says. "I heard that from here."

"Sorry," I say, holding my stomach. Well, I guess one part of my dream was true. I put on my gray hoodie and grab my backpack. "Let's go. We can quiz each other while we eat."

By the time we get to the cafeteria, it's an absolute madhouse. Usually, most kids skip breakfast, but clearly, the whole school decided to fuel up before facing their exams. We scan the room but can't find our section through the throng of students stuffing their faces and flipping through their textbooks.

"There they are," Rage says, nodding towards the back.

We weave through the crowd until we find the rest of the Monstrosities in various degrees of distress. Kat and Stanphibian look like they don't have a care in the world, Hairball is rapidly paging through his notes, and Aura has her nose in her Monsterology book, barking questions at a seemingly empty seat across from her.

"What type of metal injures vampires?" she asks.

"Excuse me?" I say, putting my backpack on the table.

"Relax, Bram," Aura says. "I'm quizzing InvisiBill. Questions like this are sure to be on Professor Holmwood's exam. Right, InvisiBill?"

"Um, right," InvisiBill says, his voice coming from the empty seat. "That's an easy one. It's copper."

"No, InvisiBill," Aura says, clearly annoyed. "We already went over this three times. It's not copper, it's silver. Don't you remember? Weapons made of one hundred percent pure silver can mortally injure a vampire by purifying the vampiric virus within their cells. Now, how many types of doppelgangers are there?"

"Uh, one," he answers.

"Nope," Aura says, furrowing her eyebrows. "Didn't you do any of the extra reading I recommended? You've gotten every question wrong."

"I studied," he says. "Some."

"How about you, Bram?" Aura asks, closing her book in frustration. "Did you study?"

"Of course," I say, "but probably not as much as you."

"No one studies more than she does," Hairball says. "It's like a disease."

"Very funny," Aura says. "I strive to do my best. Is there anything wrong with that?"

"Not at all," Kat says, lapping up some milk. "I wish I'd been here long enough to take the exams. Studying makes me feel like a normal kid. But instead, I'm stuck at Monster House while you guys take your exams."

"What's wrong with girls anyway?" Hairball asks.

"We're just smarter," Aura says. "Isn't it obvious?"

"I'm not touching that one," I say. "I'm gonna get some food. I'm starving."

As I make my way over to the buffet, I grab a plate and start loading it with red food, like tomatoes, red peppers, and beets. Just then, a cafeteria imp flutters by and offers me a plate of Swedish Fish.

"Gee, thanks," I say, popping one into my mouth.

But as soon as I chew it, the imp giggles, and I realize it tastes nothing like Swedish Fish. In fact, it sort of tastes like... liver? Gross!

But as I spit it into the trash, I hear—

"Good luck today, Fang Face."

One

I turn around to find Harpoon and the other Howlers standing behind me. Blobby squeezes his head beneath the buffet sneeze guard and starts swallowing all of the hamburger patties. Well, that's utterly disgusting.

"Um, thanks," I say. "You too."

"You know," Harpoon says, with a sly smile, "I overheard Professor Hexum telling Professor Morris that he has a special test just for you."

"Um, what?" I say, my head spinning.

Is she serious? Why would Hexum be giving me a 'special' test? What does that even mean? Is she messing with me? I wouldn't put it past her.

"You heard me," Harpoon says. "Enjoy your Survival Skills exam. I know we'll enjoy watching you. C'mon, Howlers. Let's go."

As the Howlers walk away cackling, Blobby scarfs down a whole tray of prepackaged jelly cups, forms into a big ball of flesh, and rolls after them. Meanwhile, I've pretty much lost my appetite.

I find my way back to our table and sit down.

No matter how hard I try, I can't get Harpoon's comment out of my head. I mean, Hexum is a mentalist. He could embarrass me a million ways to Sunday.

Ugh, what's he going to do to me?

"You okay?" Kat asks. "You're not eating anything and you look a little shell-shocked."

"I'm fine," I say, lying through my teeth.

"Great," Aura says, standing up. "Because our first

exam starts in ten minutes."

Awesome.

I can't wait.

CHAPTER TWO

SCHOOL DAZE

My mind is totally muddled.

I mean, between my nightmare about Johnny and Harpoon's breakfast bombshell about my 'special' test with Hexum, I'm totally off my game.

My first exam disaster is in Professor Holmwood's Monsterology class. I worked hard all semester to learn the various monster categories and characteristics so the test should have been a breeze. But instead, I'm struggling to remember the difference between a chimera and a chupacabra and a kelpie versus a kobold.

Time seems to stand still and I find myself staring off into space when, all of a sudden, the bell rings ending class. While the other kids hand in their exams with big smiles on their faces, I'm feeling depressed. And I'm not the only one disappointed with my submission.

"Bram, is everything okay?" Professor Holmwood asks, looking at both sides of my paper. "The second page of your exam is completely blank."

"What?" I say, peering over. "Oh, well, look at that. I

Two

didn't even know there was a second page. Sorry, I-I guess it was harder than I thought."

"I would say so," she says, reviewing the page I did manage to fill out. "This is very unlike you, Bram. You're one of my strongest students and know this material inside and out. Tell me, what's a wraith?"

"A wraith?" I say. "That's easy. A wraith is a type of spirit who still has business in the mortal realm."

"That is correct," Professor Holmwood says. "Yet, here you mistook a wraith for a wight."

"I did?" I say, looking at my paper. "Oh, wow, I don't know what I was thinking."

"This is your final exam, Bram," she says. "It's a big part of your overall grade. I suggest you focus harder on your remaining exams. I don't think you want to be left behind."

She's right about that.

But things just go downhill from there.

My next class is Supernatural History 101 with Professor Seward who is notorious for asking impossible essay questions. Sadly, he lives up to his reputation and asks us to answer this doozy: Throughout history, monsters have been persecuted by man. In no less than ten pages, describe five time periods in history where man sought to stamp out the existence of monsters.

Um, no less than—gulp—ten pages?

As soon as Seward says 'begin,' it's like a cannon is shot off in our classroom because everyone starts writing at a frantic pace. I put pen to paper but find myself moving way slower than my classmates. In fact, I'm having a hard time concentrating at all.

I remember the Werewolf Inquisition of the 1200s, but that's about it. I write as much as I can recall about that period and then find myself counting the blank lines in my essay book until the bell once again puts me out of my misery.

Fortunately, we hand in our booklets closed so Professor Seward can't see how little I've written. I'm pretty sure I gutted out three pages but that's all I could manage. No matter how hard I try, I can't stop thinking about Johnny's face in my dream and what Hexum has in store for me.

Thankfully, it's time for lunch.

"How did you guys do on Professor Holmwood's exam?" Aura asks, looking at her Paranormal Science textbook. Since she doesn't need to eat I guess she's doing some extra studying. Not that she needs it.

"Okay," Hairball says, cutting into a thick, raw steak. "At first, the abnormals section threw me off, but then I got into a groove. How'd you do Stan?"

"So-so," Stanphibian says, sipping a bowl of green algae through a straw.

"Great," Aura asks. "Now for the big question. InvisiBill, how did you do?"

"Oh, I blew chunks on that one," InvisiBill says from the empty seat across from her. "Major chunks."

Two

I turn away as he takes a big bite of his hamburger and starts chewing it up. So disgusting.

"I hope you did better than that," Aura says. "Do you really want to take Holmwood's class over again?"

"Yes," Stanphibian answers for him.

"Shut it, Stan," InvisiBill says.

"Crush on teacher," Stanphibian adds.

"I said shut it!" InvisiBill repeats.

"Well, I think I did well on that one," Rage says, talking with a mouth full of meatball. "I finished with enough time to double-check my answers. What about you, Bram? I bet you killed it."

"Next question," I say.

"Seriously?" Rage says. "What happened?"

But instead of answering, I look up to see the Howlers staring at me from a few tables over. Harpoon waves at me with her fork.

"No comment," I say, biting my cheese-less pizza.

"I'm sure you did better than you think," he says.

"Professor Seward's exam was like running a marathon," Aura says. "I started writing from the second he handed out the booklets to the second the bell rang."

"My paw still hurts," Hairball says, shaking his furry wrist. "I thought I was gonna run out of ink."

"What did you write about?" Rage asks Aura.

"I gave seven examples of monsters being persecuted through the ages," Aura says casually.

"Seven?" InvisiBill says. "That's funny, I did the

same thing. Minus five."

Great. Even InvisiBill did better than me.

"You know," Aura says, "as I was writing, I thought it was ironic how humans have always tried to get rid of monsters, yet here we are being trained to save humankind. Kind of makes you wonder who the real monsters are?"

"Hey, guys," Kat says, sliding into our table with a tray full of fish. "How are the exams going?"

"Painfully," InvisiBill says.

"I sure wish I was with you," Kat says. "I've been twiddling my tail and watching TV all morning."

"The horror!" InvisiBill says sarcastically.

"It's boring," she says. "Believe me, I'd rather be challenging myself with the tests you guys are taking."

Just then, the bell rings ending lunch. I take a deep breath and exhale. Our next exam is Paranormal Science, and then we see Hexum.

Harpoon smiles as she exits and my stomach drops.

"Time to go," Aura says, floating from the bench.

"Good luck," Kat says, waving from the table.

I have a distinct feeling I'm gonna need more than luck, and boy am I right. For our Paranormal Science exam, Professor Morris asks us to solve a super-complicated case study about a bank robbery involving a gang of Supernatural suspects.

As part of the exam, we're handed a huge packet of information about the crime, including pages of

Two

statements from eyewitnesses. Then, we're supposed to write all the steps we would take to conduct a proper Supernatural crime scene investigation and our conclusion as to who committed the crime. It's interesting but there's so much evidence to sort through it's taking forever.

After a while, I get a headache so I take a look around. Aura is reading, Rage is writing intensely, Hairball is pulling his hair out, Stanphibian is staring into space, and there are dozens of crumpled up papers near InvisiBill's seat. Then, my eyes meet Harpoon's and she makes a throat-cutting signal with her pencil.

Lovely.

I get back to work, but by the time I've narrowed it down to three possible suspects, the bell goes off again! I quickly scribble down my guess as to who did it and then hand in my work. It's not until we head out that I realize how wrong I was.

"Well, that was easy," Aura says. "The troll was the culprit. The giant footprints inside the bank vault were a dead giveaway."

"Yeah," Rage says. "I had the troll also. The footprints were too obvious. What about you, Bram?"

"Wait, there were footprints?" I say. "Well, um, I must have missed that part. I thought the ghost did it."

"The ghost?" Aura says, looking at me like I have three heads. "Bram, how could the ghost have done it? I'm a ghost. Do you see me leaving footprints all over the place?"

"Well, um," I stammer. "No. Not really."

"Exactly," she says. "I don't know what's wrong with you, but there's only one exam left this term. You better nail it."

Right. Except the odds of me nailing anything related to Hexum are pretty much zero to none. Hexum's class is called Survival Skills for a reason. It's all about thinking and acting—the quicker the better. And if you're not quick enough, well, you'll be lucky to get out alive.

As we enter the gymnasium everyone goes silent. We place our backpacks against the wall and fan out shoulder-to-shoulder. Hexum stands in the center of the gym, staring us down with his arms behind his back.

It's strange seeing him without his walking stick, but I'm still shocked it was really the Spear of Darkness all along. I've got to hand it to Hexum, he kept it hidden in plain sight for years. I'm just glad Van Helsing tucked it away so we don't have to think about it again.

I'd say no one embodies the Van Helsing Academy motto of 'You Must Believe in Things You Cannot Imagine' better than Hexum. So, needless to say, there's no telling what's about to happen.

And that's what worries me.

"Welcome, students," Hexum says, sounding unusually chipper as he walks down the line. "Welcome to the most joyous day of the year. Because today you will either prove that you have learned all of the material we

Two

have studied, or you will fail miserably. The rules for the exam are simple. Rule number one, do your best. Anything less will result in failure. Rule number two, no exam will be alike. Each of you will experience an exam personally tailored to you. Rule number three, everyone will take their exam simultaneously. And finally, rule number four, be prepared, because this exam will push you to the edge."

Then, he stops in front of me.

"And some of you will break."

I swallow hard.

What's that supposed to mean?

"Please ensure there is ample space between you and the students to either side of you," Hexum says.

I look right to find Rage, who slides over with a nervous smile. Then, I turn left to find a pair of yellow eyes staring back at me. It's Harpoon!

"I wanted to get close enough to hear you scream," she whispers.

"How thoughtful," I whisper back.

"Silence, Mr. Murray!" Hexum barks.

I look at Harpoon who sticks out her tongue.

Nice.

"Now, close your eyes," Hexum says. "You are to keep them closed for the duration of the class, even if your exam ends prematurely."

I close my eyes.

"Your exam will begin now," Hexum says, his voice

echoing inside my head.

Suddenly, I'm standing in the middle of a dark chamber with stone walls, a low ceiling, and no windows. I don't know what I'm doing here, but when I breathe in the air tastes stale and musty.

Just then, a large object appears.

It's a black, wooden box, tapered at both ends and covered with a lid.

My heart skips a beat.

It's... a coffin!

As my mind jumps to what might be lying inside I have an overwhelming feeling of dread. Could it be a dead body? A zombie? I scan the chamber for a way out, but I don't see a door anywhere. I'm trapped!

CRRREEEAAAK!

What's that noise?

Then, I see the lid of the coffin opening!

The next thing I know, a pale hand emerges and latches onto the side of the coffin! I jump back as shivers shoot down my spine. What is that thing?

And then it hits me.

I-I know whose hand that is!

Holy cow!

It's Count Dracula!

And there's nowhere to run!

I'm gonna have to fight him! B-But I'm not ready!

He's going to kill me!

STOP!

Two

What?

That was a girl's voice! I look around to see where it came from, and as the background of the chamber suddenly shifts back to the gymnasium, I see Kat standing there with panic in her eyes.

"What are you doing here?" Hexum yells, striding up to her with his arms crossed.

"I-I'm sorry, Professor," she says. "But something terrible just happened."

"What is it, child?" Hexum demands, looming over her. "What could be so terrible you needed to interrupt my exam?"

"I-It's the Dark Ones," Kat says. "I-I was watching the news, and the Dark Ones just attacked New York City! They're… turning people into evil monsters!"

CLASSIFIED

Person(s) of Interest

CODE NAME: NONE

REAL NAME: LUCY HOLMWOOD

BASE OF OPERATIONS: VAN HELSING ACADEMY

FACTS: Lucy Holmwood is the tenured professor of Monsterology at the Van Helsing Academy. She is a multiple award-winning biologist and is widely considered to be the leading expert in the field of Monster Species Classification. She is a trusted confidante of Lothar Van Helsing.

FIELD OBSERVATIONS:

- Highly intelligent
- Dedicated to her students
- Use extreme caution when tracking as she is quick to notice new patterns or unusual behaviors

Category: Natural
Sub-Type: None
Height: 5'5"
Weight: 145 lbs

STATUS: ACTIVE TARGET

DEPARTMENT OF SUPERNATURAL INVESTIGATIONS

CHAPTER THREE

MONSTERS UNLEASHED

I would have taken any excuse to get out of Hexum's exam, but not this.

I mean, the Dark Ones are attacking New York City! After Kat crashed class, Hexum postponed his exam and immediately went to find Van Helsing. Once he left the gymnasium, the rest of us dashed over to Monster House to catch the news on TV. There's probably thirty of us smushed in the common room.

"Ugh, what's that?" Hairball complains.

"It smells like rotten fish sticks," InvisiBill says.

"Sorry," Stanphibian says.

"Quiet!" Aura shouts. "Turn on the TV."

"On it," Kat says, grabbing the remote control.

Just then, the TV flicks on and my jaw drops because I can't believe what I'm seeing. Monsters are all over the city! Werewolves are prowling the subway system, zombies are lumbering through Times Square, and winged creatures are flying around the Empire State Building!

"What are those things?" InvisiBill asks.

"Gargoyles," Rage says. "You really did flunk Professor Holmwood's exam, didn't you?"

"Shush!" Aura orders. "Turn up the volume. Everyone be quiet!"

Well, she doesn't have to worry about me because I'm absolutely speechless right now. I've never seen so many monsters in public before. There must be hundreds of them and watching them attack innocent civilians is horrifying.

Those poor people. One minute they were going about their day, and the next they're running for their lives. They don't stand a chance against these evil monsters.

"… city is in ruins," a female news anchor says, as the volume increases and the screen flips from one horrible scene to the next. "There is nowhere to run. Nowhere to hide. The police are doing their best to mount a response, but they are simply not equipped to deal with this… this barrage of terror. We remind you again to stay indoors. Bar your doors and windows. Do not, I repeat, do not let a werewolf or zombie bite you. The President has declared a state of emergency and the military is on their way. But will it be enough to—. Wait. Please hold on, this just in… I'm now being handed a letter, written… in blood? It's from Count Dracula himself. The letter is addressed to all world leaders, and it says…"

Three

"Turn it off," comes a voice from the back of the room, startling everyone.

Kat immediately clicks off the TV, and when we turn around we find Van Helsing standing in the doorway with Crawler, Professor Morris, and Professor Hexum behind him. And Van Helsing is holding a letter of his own.

"I will read you the correspondence myself," Van Helsing says, snapping the paper taut. "To all Naturals. Be warned, for what is happening in New York City is a small demonstration of my power. For far too long your kind has hunted my kind to the brink of extinction. But now it is your turn to experience what it is like to be hunted. I have returned to fulfill my destiny and lead my army of Dark Ones to destroy you. Prepare yourselves… if you can. Your Master, Count Dracula."

"Um, what's that supposed to mean?" Hairball asks.

"It means the war has finally begun," Van Helsing says. "The war between monsters and men."

Suddenly, a chill runs down my spine.

"Students," Van Helsing continues. "we are facing the most dangerous foe in the history of the human race. Count Dracula intends to rule over the entire population of Earth, and he has never been so bold. Billions of lives are at stake, and if Count Dracula succeeds those lives will not only perish, but their undead souls will join the ranks of the Dark Ones."

"We've got to stop him!" Aura says.

"No," Van Helsing says. "There is no 'we.' It is far

too dangerous and you are not ready for a threat of this magnitude. All of you will remain here under the Supernatural protection of the Artifacts of Virtue. No one is to leave campus for any reason. Is that clear?"

"Yes," we respond in unison.

"Very good," he says. "But as an added precaution, I have called upon Mrs. Clops to look after you—some of you more than others."

Not surprisingly, he's staring at our section.

"I must travel to New York City to put an end to this madness," he says, raising his Crossbow of Purity. "Several of the professors will be joining me on this mission, but Professor Seward and Dr. Hagella will join Mrs. Clops and remain here at the academy. I am relying on all of you to keep your word. It is extremely dangerous out there, and if you venture beyond these gates there is no telling what may happen to you."

I swallow hard.

Van Helsing stares everyone down, ending on me.

"Please, I implore you," he says. "Heed my warning."

And then he turns and exits the common room, followed by Crawler, Morris, and Hexum.

Once he's gone, we all look at each other wide-eyed, but nobody says a word.

***

What's happening in New York City is bad enough,

Three

but not being able to do anything about it feels even worse. Especially since we've been stuck in the common room for hours under the watchful eye of Vi Clops, our resident cyclops, and Monster House manager.

"This is so frustrating," I whisper to Hairball.

"Yeah," he whispers back. "Everything is going nuts out there and we're not even allowed to fight."

"Quiet yer selves down," Vi Clops grunts, her giant eyeball shifting between Hairball and me. She's sitting on the floor with her back against the doorframe, forming a twenty-foot tall barricade. "No one is leavin' here unless yer bein' carried out on a stretcher."

Well, that's pleasant.

After another ten minutes or so of silence, Vi Clops rubs her eye and Kat leans over.

"I still don't understand why she's babysitting us," Kat whispers. "How come the Howlers aren't being forced to sit here until Van Helsing gets back?"

"Because they haven't snuck off of campus before," I whisper back. "I know you're new here but our team has a reputation for leaving school grounds without permission. Van Helsing doesn't trust us to listen to him and actually stay put."

"I wouldn't trust us either," Hairball says, stretching out in his tiny chair. "I wouldn't trust us at all."

"Same," Stanphibian adds.

"No talkin'!" Vi Clops snipes.

Everyone clams up.

Then, Aura floats a little closer to me.

"We've got to get out of here," she whispers.

"No kidding," I whisper back.

"No, I mean we've really got to get out of here," she whispers more urgently. "A while ago I received an alert from the spirit network. A cargo ship just arrived at the port."

"Um, okay," I whisper, totally confused. "Don't ships arrive at the port all the time?"

"No," she whispers. "You don't get it. This ship is unusual. It came from Romania and is carrying cargo from Bucharest."

"So?" I whisper.

"So," she whispers. "Don't you know your geography? Bucharest is the capital of Romania, and it's located in a region called Wallachia."

Wallachia?

Why does that name sound so familiar?

"Do I really have to spell it out for you?" she whispers. "Wallachia was Vlad Dracul's kingdom. Count Dracula is from Wallachia."

"Quiet!" Vi Clops barks.

Holy cow! She's right!

I look at Aura, my eyes bugging out, and she nods in acknowledgment. Now I remember. Wallachia is where Vlad Dracul's men used the original Blood Grail to turn him into Count Dracula. So, if a ship is coming from Wallachia, it could be carrying supplies from Count

Three

Dracula's homeland. Supplies he'll use to take over the world!

I wait for Vi Clops to look away, and then whisper—

"We've got to get to that ship."

"Ya' think, dummy?" Aura whispers back. "But don't worry, I'm on it. I already put InvisiBill on the case."

"InvisiBill?" I whisper. "Are you nuts?"

"Probably," she whispers. "But he's the only one who can get in and out of here without being seen."

Well, she's right about that. And come to think of it, I haven't heard his annoying voice in a while. I wonder what he's been—

"Delivery!"

Huh? That came from the hall.

Suddenly, a dozen pizza boxes stacked sky-high march through the common room door. But the thing is, there's no one carrying them.! That's when everything clicks. It's InvisiBill, and he ordered pizza.

My stomach rumbles as the delicious smell wafts through the common room. But why is InvisiBill bringing in pizza? Then, it clicks. Aura is a genius.

"What's this?" Vi Clops says, licking her chops.

"Dinner," InvisiBill says, placing the stack of boxes in front of her. "You looked hungry so I took the liberty of ordering you a few snacks."

"Yer violatin' the rules," Vi Clops says, looking around for InvisiBill. "But I am hungry. We'll talk later."

She rips the top off the first box, grabs the entire

pizza with one giant hand, and woofs it down in one bite. Then, she moves on to the next box.

"Um, what's going on?" Kat asks. "Because I really can't unsee this."

"Vi Clops is a cyclops," I whisper. "And all cyclops pass out after they've eaten a big meal. So, it's just a matter of time before we're outta here."

"Well, then," Kat says, positioning her chair to face Vi Clops. "I guess this is worth watching after all."

A minute later, Vi Clops has finished eating.

"Just what I needed," she says, her big eye closing slowly. "Yer all jus' stay here."

"Shame to miss out on all that pizza," Hairball says. "But it was for a good cause."

"I guess I could have saved a pie for you guys," InvisiBill says.

"Yeah," Rage says. "That would have been nice."

"Sorry," InvisiBill says. "Well, at least I had one before I came in."

"What?" Rage says.

"Shhh!" Aura whispers. "Look, she's going down."

Just then, Vi Clops' eyelid closes and her head tilts to the side. Then, she starts snoring like a buzz saw.

"Okay, let's go," Hairball whispers. "But walk softly."

We carefully squeeze past Vi Clops one-by-one. Of course, Stanphibian trips and nearly falls on top of her, but thanks to Kat's catlike reflexes, she catches him just

Three

in time. Then, we book down the stairs into the foyer.

Fortunately, no one else is around.

"It sure is dark," Rage says, looking out the window. "It feels like we were trapped in there forever."

"What now?" Kat asks.

"Now we've got a ship to catch," Aura says. "We need to see what cargo came on that boat."

"Do you really think that's a good idea?" Rage asks. "You heard Van Helsing. He told us not to leave campus. Besides, every time we go off school grounds someone nearly eats it."

"Look, I know it's scary," Aura says, "but Count Dracula is attacking New York City. We've got to do whatever we can to help. Right, Bram?"

I open my mouth to answer but nothing comes out.

I mean, they're both right. Every time we leave campus something bad happens. But if we don't see what's on that boat, we may let Count Dracula get exactly what he needs to win his war against humanity.

And the worst part is it's all my fault.

Count Dracula only exists because of me.

If Professor Faustius didn't use me as the Blood Grail this whole nightmare never would have happened.

"Bram?" Aura repeats.

"Um, yeah," I say finally. "Aura's right. We've got to see what's on that boat. It might be important to stop Count Dracula."

"Okay," Kat says. "I'm always ready to mix it up. But

how will we get to this port anyway? It's not like any of us are old enough to drive."

"Don't sweat it," Hairball says. "I'll drive us there."

"Oh," Kat says, "do you have a driver's license?"

"Nope," he says, smoothing his hairy mustache. "I just look the part. Let's roll."

"Oh, no," Rage says, his head in his hands. "This might be worse than facing Count Dracula."

Three

CLASSIFIED

Person(s) of Interest

CODE NAME: NONE

REAL NAME: QUINCY MORRIS IV

BASE OF OPERATIONS: VAN HELSING ACADEMY

FACTS: Quincy Morris IV is the tenured professor of Paranormal Science at the Van Helsing Academy. He is a former Sergeant with the Texas Rangers and is the leading expert in the field of Supernatural Crime Scene Investigations. He is a trusted advisor of Lothar Van Helsing.

FIELD OBSERVATIONS:

- High technical acumen
- Patented new technology to track Supernatural criminals
- Uses 'unorthodox' techniques to solve difficult cases
- Armed and Dangerous

Category: Natural
Sub-Type: None
Height: 6'2"
Weight: 193 lbs

STATUS: ACTIVE TARGET

DEPARTMENT OF SUPERNATURAL INVESTIGATIONS

CHAPTER FOUR

GIVE ME THE DIRT

Remind me to never, ever, E-V-E-R get into a vehicle Hairball's driving again.

This time we swiped Crawler's bus from the garage, and even though Hairball managed not to turn us into roadkill, he certainly did his darndest to try. First, he nearly smashed through the front gates of the academy. Then, he almost caused a twelve-car pileup on the highway. And last, but not least, he flew by a cop going way over the speed limit.

So, yeah, I'm done with that.

And I'm not the only one.

"Stop the bus!" Rage calls out. "I've gotta puke."

"Seriously?" Hairball says, pulling to the side of the road. "Did you eat something that didn't agree with you?"

"No, you idiot," Rage says, running down the aisle holding his stomach. "Your stupid driving doesn't agree with me. Now open the door."

"Backseat driver," Hairball says, opening the folding door. "There's always a backseat driver."

Four

Rage hops out and tosses his cookies in the bushes.

"I know how he feels," Kat says, looking green herself. "Someone should ban Hairball from ever driving again."

"Well, this is actually a good place to stop," Aura says, looking out the windshield. "The port is a few miles up the road. Hairball, turn off the engine and kill the headlights. We don't want anyone to know we're here."

"Yes, sir," Hairball says, shutting off the engine.

"What now?" I ask.

"Now we need to find the cargo ship," Aura says. "It's dark and foggy which should help us stay hidden, but we need to get the lay of the land."

"Leave it to me," I say, stepping off the bus. "Dark and foggy is my specialty. See you in a few minutes. Feel better, Rage."

Rage is still bent over but manages to wave goodbye.

I concentrate on one thought—become a bat—and then transform and take flight. I figure the best way to see everything is from up high. But Aura is right, the fog is so thick I need to stay focused. The last thing I need is to screw up my sonar and crash into the side of a ship.

I reach a comfortable altitude and take in the scene. The port itself is massive, serving as a transportation hub between land and sea. On land, there are a bunch of large warehouses that all look the same—long and low with trucks parked in the loading zones. On the sea, several wooden piers jut into the water for ships to dock.

It's an impressive complex, but I'm not here for a grand tour of the place. We need to find Count Dracula's cargo, but I notice a few problems that will make that easier said than done.

For instance, there are actually three ships docked here, so we'll need to figure out which one came from Wallachia. There are also a bunch of armed guards patrolling the place, so this isn't going to be a cakewalk. I just don't see how we'll get everyone inside the port without being seen. Especially with knuckleheads like Stanphibian and Hairball.

I think I've got all the intel I need, so I head back. When I reach the bus, I see Rage still crouched near the bushes, so I touch down next to him.

"Ahh!" Rage screams, startled. "What's wrong with you? You scared me half to death."

"Sorry," I say, turning back to kid-form. "Are you done yakking?"

"Yeah," he says, wiping his chin. "I think so. Although I considered saving some for Hairball."

"Shhh!" Aura whispers, phasing through the side of the bus. "Do you want to get us discovered?"

"No," I say. "But we're going to need a plan so we don't get shot."

I run the team through everything I saw and after much debate, we come up with a plan. Finding the cargo will require stealth so we can't take everybody. Based on our abilities, we eventually decide that Aura, InvisiBill,

Four

and I are best suited for the job. Each of us will sneak into the port on our own and explore one of the ships.

Aura will take the ship farthest away, I'll take the one in the middle, and InvisiBill will take the one closest to the entrance. I'm a little nervous about giving InvisiBill such a big responsibility, but it's not like we have better options.

"Don't worry," he says. "I've got it."

"You better," Aura says. "Now the rest of you stay put or you'll answer to me. Is that clear?"

"Crystal," Rage says, swallowing hard.

"Okay," she says. "Let's do this."

I go back to bat-form, but as soon as I take off, I hear—

"Oof!" Stanphibian yelps.

"What happened?" Kat asks.

"Stan slipped," Hairball says. "Yuck, what's on the bottom of his flipper?"

"My barf," Rage says.

I shake my head. I'll be amazed if those bozos manage not to get caught. Anyway, I can't worry about them now, I have my own issues to deal with. I flap my way into the fog and glide over the port entrance. Looking down, I see two armed guards talking to one another. Fortunately, they have no idea I'm up here.

I keep flying until I'm directly over my target docked at the center pier. For the first time, I realize the ship is really big. From here it looks like it's half the size of a football field, with a tall bridge, and a bunch of crates stacked on the rear deck.

Well, that must be the cargo.

I circle and do a quick count. There must be twenty crates in total. I need to figure out what's inside, but how?

Just then, I see two deckhands heading my way. This could be my chance to get some info. But as I descend towards them, I'm not sure I'm in the best form for stealth mode. After all, I don't want them to freak out if they see a bat hanging over their shoulder. So, I transform into a mist, blending into the fog over their heads.

As the wind picks up, I realize I need to concentrate just to keep my molecules together. Then, the men show up and start removing the ropes that fasten the crates to the deck. One of them has dark hair and the other is wearing a gray, knit cap.

"Worst job we've ever had," the dark-haired man says, untying a knot. "Now I know why 'ole Sam refused to do the second run. I nearly broke my back lifting those crates."

"Nearly?" the man with the cap says. "I think Tommy broke his. The poor guy can't even get out of bed. To think, we got all of those things on the ship and now we have to get 'em off."

"We need equipment to get these off," the dark-haired man says. "I don't care how much that guy paid us, it took six of us to carry one crate and I've never lifted anythin' so heavy in my life."

Four

"The guy gave me the creeps, too," the man with the cap says. "Barely said a word. And you couldn't see his eyes beneath the shadows of his hat. I don't trust people who don't look you in the eyes. And there was somethin' else. I didn't want to say nothin' at the time, but I swear he carried ten of these crates all by himself. One second they were sittin' on the dock, and the next thing I know they're sittin' on the ship. Did you see that?"

"I did," the dark-haired man says. "But I thought I was crazy. I don't know about you, but if I never see that guy again I'll be just fine."

"Wouldn't it be nice to know what we were carryin' though?" the man with the cap asks. "What do you think is inside these boxes?"

"I don't know and I don't care," the dark-haired man says. "To me, it smells like somethin's rotting in there. I just want to get 'em off our ship and be done with the whole thing. But I do know one thing. I'm never takin' a job from Romania again."

"I agree with that," the man with the knit cap says.

Romania?

That's it! This is the ship!

The two men untie the ropes on the last crate and head back towards the other end of the ship. If I'm going to find out what's inside this might be my only chance! I wait a few minutes to make sure they're gone and then transform back into a kid. Even though we're docked I need to steady my feet as the ship rocks back and forth on the water.

I wish Aura was here to help, but I'll just have to finish my investigation and head back to the bus to share what I've learned.

If I heard the deckhands right, this is actually the second delivery from Romania. If that's the case, then Count Dracula may already have some of what he needs from his homeland. And when they were talking about that creepy guy, I realized there's only one person who fits that description—Count Dracula himself!

I peer around the crate to make sure the coast is clear and then get to work. The crate itself is big and rectangular. It's a few feet taller than me and probably seven feet wide. I can see why it would take six men to lift one of these things. Just for fun, I try lifting it but it doesn't budge.

Note to self: I may be half-vampire but I don't have even half of Count Dracula's strength.

Now, how do I get this thing open?

I look around the outside of the crate and realize it's bolted shut by metal clips. To get inside I'll need a tool to pry those clips off. Then, I spot a crowbar leaning against one of the crates.

Bingo!

I grab the crowbar and move to the crate on the end. I shove the crowbar beneath one of the metal clips and push down, putting all of my weight behind it. After a good struggle, the clip pops off. I repeat this process all

Four

the way around until the entire panel is loose, and then I remove it.

To my surprise, inside the crate is another large, wooden box. Suddenly, my nostrils are flooded by a horrible stench! Man, that guy wasn't kidding. Whatever's inside that box smells like it's well past its due date!

In fact, the smell is so noxious it's making me lightheaded. But I'm too close to stop now. I need to find out what's inside this box. So, I grab my crowbar and explore the outside of the wooden box.

This time there aren't any metal clips to deal with, but there are plenty of wood planks. So, I brace myself for the smell and push the crowbar into a seam. I pull down hard, popping a plank from the end of the box, and the smell hits me full force.

I stumble back, feeling kind of woozy when—

"Hey," comes a girl's voice from behind me.

I jump out of my skin, somehow managing not to scream my lungs out. And when I turn around, Aura is phasing up through the deck of the ship.

"Didn't you just yell at me for freaking out Rage?" I whisper. "You could've blown the whole thing."

"Sorry," she whispers, covering her mouth. "I guess I'm not perfect either. My ship wasn't the one we're looking for. What do you have here?"

"This is it," I whisper. "This ship just arrived from Romania. And according to the men on board, Count Dracula himself helped them load these smelly crates onto the vessel. The smell is actually making me dizzy."

"Really? I can't smell anything," Aura says. "It's one of the drawbacks of being a ghost. What's it smell like?"

"Death," I whisper. "Now can you stop talking so we can look inside?"

"Yeah," she says. "Let's do it."

I pinch my nose and we both lean forward, poking our heads through the opening. But when I see what's inside my jaw drops because it doesn't make any sense.

"It's just... dirt?" Aura says. "Lots and lots of dirt."

"Foul-smelling dirt," I say.

Then, I see little white specks wiggling around inside.

"Oh, yuck," I say. "It's filled with maggots."

"Thank goodness I can't throw up," Aura says, backing out of the crate. "Because that's really, really disgusting."

"Yeah," I say, pulling my head out. I don't think I could take a second more. "But I don't get it. Why is Count Dracula shipping boxes of dirt from Romania to America? There's dirt here too."

"But it's not just from Romania," Aura says. "It's from Wallachia. His kingdom."

"Yep," I say. "And the men said all the crates are like this one."

"This is so weird," Aura says. "We should probably go back and tell the others. And speaking of others, where's InvisiBill? That moron better not have been—"

"FREEZE!" squawks a loud voice from overhead.

Four

What?

Suddenly, I hear FWOOP FWOOP noises, and when I look up there's a squad of helicopters flying in the sky, shining spotlights on us!

Then, I notice the initials 'D.S.I.' painted in black on the side of one of the helicopters.

"What's going on?" I say.

Just then, the helicopter above us lowers a long, black tube attached to a big, brown bag.

"Bram, run!" Aura says.

But before I can move, there's a loud SUCKING noise, and the next thing I know, Aura is vacuumed into the tube!

"Aura!" I yell.

"DON'T MOVE, MONSTER!"

Monster?

I've got to get out of here!

But just as I take a step, a clear tube drops from the sky, trapping me inside! And then a pink mist fills the tube, making me gag!

What is this stuff? It smells like sulfur!

I try pushing the tube over but it won't budge.

And suddenly, I feel... super tired.

I try... keeping my eyes open but I can't.

And then everything goes dark.

CHAPTER FIVE

AGENT M

I wake up in a haze.

I'm lying on a cold floor and my limbs feel like they weigh a thousand pounds each. There's drool running down my chin and it takes everything I have just to wipe it away with my sleeve. I don't know what that pink stuff was that knocked me out, but boy it's powerful stuff.

I blink my eyes a few times until my vision clears, and that's when I realize I'm in a small, concrete room that looks like it belongs in a dungeon. And apparently, I'm still trapped inside that giant, glass tube those helicopters dropped on me at the port.

Well, this certainly isn't the Holiday Inn.

Where the heck am I anyway? I press my hand against the glass and pull myself up to my feet. Okay, I guess it doesn't matter where I am. The real question is, how am I going to get out of here?

Suddenly, a loud CLICK echoes through the room, and when I spin around I'm blinded by a bright light! I shield my eyes when I realize it's not only bright but

Five

incredibly hot.

It's burning my skin!

"Good evening, 'Brampire,'" comes a woman's voice.

"Who are you?" I ask.

I try focusing on her face, but it's impossible to see through the intense light. Besides, I have to cover my face with the hoodie so I don't burn to death! I don't know how much more I can take!

"P-Please," I plead. "Turn it off!"

Then, the light clicks off and I feel immediate relief. I look at the back of my hands and they're bright red.

"Sorry, Brampire," the woman says. "Just taking some precautions."

"H-How do you know my name?" I ask, but when I look her way I'm still seeing spots.

"Well, it is written right there on your shiny badge," she says. "But we didn't need the help because we've been watching you for quite a while."

Just then, the light goes on again and I flinch, but this time it's way less glaring and there's no heat.

"I'll introduce myself," she continues, and when she steps forward I can finally see her face, but she doesn't look anything like I expect. She's super tall, with red, spikey hair, a square jaw, and piercing blue eyes. She's wearing a crisp, black suit with a matching tie, and she's holding up some kind of a device that looks like a high-tech flashlight, complete with blinking lights.

"You can call me Agent M," she continues. "And I

work for DSI, also known as the Department of Supernatural Investigations."

The Department of Supernatural Investigations?

Suddenly, I remember seeing the initials 'DSI' on one of the helicopters.

"Are you, like, part of the Dark Ones?" I ask.

"The Dark Ones?" she repeats. "Oh, no, no, no, my dear. We work for the government. In fact, you're now part of a very exclusive club who know we even exist. When monsters come crawling out of their holes, we get the call. So, I guess you can call us the good guys."

The good guys? Suddenly, I feel much better.

"That's great news," I say. "Because this is all a big misunderstanding. See, we're good guys, too."

"Right," she says. "You must think I just fell off the back of a turnip truck. Let's get this straight, kid. You're a monster. That makes you a bad guy."

"What?" I say. "No, I'm on your side."

"Oh, really?" she says, breaking into a smile. "Well, let's do the good guy test then. Are you a vampire?"

"Well," I say. "Technically, yes. But I'm only half—"

"Were you on Count Dracula's ship?" she presses on, not waiting for my answer.

"Well, yes," I say, and suddenly I feel like I'm being interrogated.

"So, let's summarize," she says. "You're a vampire who was captured aboard Count Dracula's ship? I have news for you, kid. You just aced the bad guy test."

Five

"Hold on," I say, "maybe we can have a do-over?"

"A do-over?" she says. "That's cute. Listen, kid, I don't think you understand what's going on here. You see, the Department of Supernatural Investigations was formed way back in the 1930s for one purpose—to protect the United States of America from monsters. You can think of us as government-employed monster hunters. We spend our entire professional lives hauling in monsters just like you. Of course, we wouldn't want to frighten innocent people so we keep it all undercover. But now that Count Dracula attacked New York City, the secret is out and my phone won't stop ringing."

Wow, for all of the Supernatural History we covered in Professor Seward's class, he never mentioned the Department of Supernatural Investigations. It must be so secret he doesn't even know about it.

"So, let's look at the facts here," Agent M continues, pacing back and forth. "Count Dracula's minions have attacked New York City, with an estimated population of—"

"Hang on," I say. "If your job is to protect the United States from monsters, then why aren't you in New York City right now? Wouldn't stopping Count Dracula be a better use of your time than grilling me?"

"Don't you worry," Agent M says. "My agents are all over the crisis in New York City. But believe it or not, Count Dracula isn't even there, so you've jumped to my number one priority. See, we were monitoring that cargo ship for a reason. We thought we'd catch Count Dracula red-handed when he came to claim his cargo. And while we didn't nab Count Dracula, we got the next best thing, his protégé, who also happens to be the only other vampire on the planet."

His protégé? Who's that?

Wait a second. She's talking about me!

"So, tell me," Agent M says. "Why do you need twenty boxes of dirt from Romania?"

"What?" I say. "I-I don't need them. I already told you, I'm not working with Count Dracula!"

"Uh-huh," she says. "Look, kid, we know this is the second shipment from Romania. What was in the first shipment? More boxes of dirt?"

"I've got no clue," I say.

"Come on," she says. "We're already tracking down where that first shipment went, so you might as well come clean. What are you and the Dark Ones up to?"

"I don't know," I say firmly. "Look, I'm not with the Dark Ones. I'm just a student at the Van Helsing Academy."

"The Van Helsing Academy," she says, rolling over a stool and sitting down. "We know all about the Van Helsing Academy. The school's charter says it's an accredited private academy dedicated to the education of extremely 'gifted' children. What it doesn't say, however, is that it's a secret organization for the next generation of Supernatural terrorists."

Five

"What?" I say. "That's not true."

"No?" Agent M says, her left eyebrow raised. "Then I'm guessing your infamous Headmaster doesn't talk about what happens to his graduates."

"What are you talking about?" I say.

"You mean, you don't know?" she says. "Tell me, haven't you ever wondered what will happen to you when you 'graduate' from the prestigious Van Helsing Academy?"

Well, come to think of it, I haven't.

And now that she's mentioned it, it's actually a great question. I mean, other than my father, I haven't heard Van Helsing talk about anyone who's left the school before. But my dad didn't even graduate, he just took off on his own.

"Um, no," I say.

"Well, let me clue you in," she says, leaning forward. "You're not going to make it. You see, Van Helsing is just setting you up for failure. He's not teaching you how to blend into society, and when monsters like you get out into the real world and struggle to fit in, well, you tend to go berserk. And do you know whose job it is to put you back in your place?"

"Um, yours?" I offer.

"See, now we're getting somewhere," Agent M says. "That's right. My agents remove dangerous monsters like you from society so ordinary citizens can live in peace."

"But then you release them, right?" I ask.

"Oh no," she says, shaking her head. "We never release monsters back into the world. That's not what we're about. Our job is to protect the public, and once we capture a monster it's for keeps. That's when the real fun begins. That's when we find out what their weaknesses are. What scares them. What makes them scream. And sometimes, what makes them die."

"Wait, what?" I say.

"You heard me," she says, lifting her flashlight. "That's how we develop things like the solar beam I'm holding here or the weapons we used to capture you and your friends at the port. We test and test and test on different monsters until we find the most effective tools to bring them down."

Holy cow! That's crazy. She's using monsters as guinea pigs to take down other monsters! But what she's saying must be true because they nabbed Aura and me in a matter of seconds.

Suddenly, I realize I have no clue where Aura is.

Or the rest of the Monstrosities.

"Where are my friends?" I demand.

"Don't worry," she says. "We've got them all. The ghost girl, the fish boy, the hairy kid, the cat girl, the little guy with glasses, even the invisible boy."

Suddenly, panic sets in. I mean, based on what she just said, she could be torturing them right now!

"Let them go," I say. "I promise, I'll do whatever you want if you just let them go."

Five

"Impressive," she says, her eyebrows raised. "A monster with character. I think that's a first. Unfortunately, I can't let your friends go. After all, we don't want anyone else getting hurt out there."

"I told you we're good monsters," I say.

"That's right," she says, tapping her index finger on her chin. "But is there really such a thing as a 'good monster?' I'm going with a 'hard no.'"

"Let me out of here!" I demand, pounding on the glass tube.

"Now there's the monster I was expecting to see," she says. "Relax, you're not going anywhere. I'm honored to have you here. We've never captured a bona fide vampire before. But here's the good news. Whatever we learn from studying you will be used to capture and destroy your leader, the King of Darkness himself. Just you wait. We're going to have all sorts of fun together."

I open my mouth to speak but stop myself. She won't believe me anyway. I've got to get out of here.

Agent M stands up and kicks her stool away.

"Listen, this has been a great conversation," she says. "But I need real answers. So, I'll give you a choice. You can either tell me the truth about your plans, or I'll bring in your friends one-by-one, and we'll see how much pain they can take."

"But...," I say, dropping to my knees. "I am telling you the truth."

"Uh-huh," Agent M says. "Sure, kid. Tell you what,

I'll give you one hour to think about what you want to do and then I'll be back. Maybe I'll bring in your ghost friend first. We've had lots of ghosts here at DSI, and I've got a pretty good idea of what makes them squeal. See you in an hour."

Then, Agent M smiles and exits the room.

I press my back against the glass and slide down until I'm sitting on the floor.

Great.

I have one hour.

And I don't know what to do.

CLASSIFIED

AGENT PERSONNEL PROFILE

AGENT DETAILS:

ROLE: DSI SUPERVISOR

REAL NAME:

AGENT NAME: AGENT M

HEIGHT: 6' 2"

HAIR COLOR: RED

EYE COLOR: GREEN

YRS OF SERVICE: 13

SPECIALTY: MONSTER HUNTING

TRAINING:
- Monster Biology
- Monster Psychology
- Monster Capture
- Firearms
- Law Enforcement

SKILLS:
- Leadership
- Risk/Threat Assessment
- Operation Planning
- Counter-Intelligence
- Effective Communication

DEPARTMENT OF SUPERNATURAL INVESTIGATIONS

CHAPTER SIX

THE GREAT ESCAPE

I'm running out of time before Agent M comes back, and I don't know what to do.

She thinks I'm in cahoots with Count Dracula, and if I don't tell her what she wants to hear she'll torture my friends one by one! The thing is, I already told her the truth and it wasn't good enough. So, at this point I'm clueless.

Ever since she left I've been walking in circles inside my glass prison, waiting for the answer to magically appear. Unfortunately, no miracles have arrived, so I guess that leaves me with two choices. Either I try pleading my case again or I start telling lies.

But the thing is, even if I do lie and tell her I'm working for Count Dracula—which I'm not—I'm sure she'll torture my friends anyway. After all, she said putting monsters in their place was her job. And she seems to really love her job.

So, that takes me to option number three. I need to bust out of here and free my friends before she gets back.

Six

I put my hands on the glass tube and push with all of my might but it doesn't budge. I pound on the glass but it's way too thick. I swipe my palm along the surface looking for a crack to mist out of, but it's perfectly smooth. Well, so much for that.

I take a deep breath and exhale. They thought of everything. In other words, it's a perfect vampire trap.

You know, I bet they were planning to put Count Dracula in here, but instead I'm the lucky one.

Awesome.

If only Van Helsing knew where we were. He'd come to rescue us. Of course, after he rescued us he'd probably kill us for sneaking off again, but he'd rescue us first.

At least, I think he would.

But who am I kidding? Van Helsing isn't coming and there's nothing I can do to save my friends. I sit down on the floor and try not to think of what's to come.

Then, something catches my eye.

There's some sort of a faint, grayish mist circling the top of the tube. It's moving incredibly fast, so fast I can barely track it as it goes around and around. I stand up to take a closer look.

What is that?

Suddenly, my alarm bells go off. I mean, what if it's one of Agent M's weapons? What if she sent this thing in to scare me into talking? What if—

But before I can finish my thought, a section of the gray mist branches off from the rest, forms a big ball, and

SLAMS into the glass tube!

The impact rocks the tube hard, knocking me off balance, and I smash my shoulder against the far side of the glass. Then, the tube teeter-totters back and forth a few times until it finally settles back down on the ground.

What just happened?

But when I look back up the gray mist is gone!

I don't see it anywhere. Was it even real?

My shoulder is still throbbing so I don't think I imagined it. But then again, I can't explain it either. I look to the spot where the mist made contact and see a crack in the glass. Well, there's the evidence.

So, I guess it was—

Wait a second!

The glass is cracked!

That means I can get out of here! I don't know who sent that mist in here but I'll have to find out later. Because right now I've got to escape before Agent M comes back. Without wasting a second, I transform into a mist and flow out of my prison.

It feels great to be free, but there's no time for a picnic. After all, who knows what DSI is doing to my friends. I've got to find them and fast!

I stay a mist and pass through the doorframe into a narrow, dingy hallway. Well, I guess DSI doesn't care for uplifting work environments. But the drab décor is the last thing on my mind because I spot three more doors with armed guards posted outside.

Six

I'm guessing my friends are behind those doors, so as long as I stay in mist-form I should be able to enter unnoticed. I cling to the ceiling, staying high above the guards' heads until I reach the first door, and then I slip inside.

I'm in a room identical to the one that held me, but instead of a glass tube there's a large, brown sack hanging from the ceiling—and it looks eerily similar to the one that sucked up Aura! And next to that is a metal table with wrist and ankle shackles.

I circle the bag but don't hear anything coming from inside. Since time is of the essence I should probably move on, yet something tells me the bag isn't empty. I don't see an opening so if I'm going to check inside I'll need something to cut it open with.

Now, where can I find something sharp?

Then, it hits me.

Duh! I've got something sharp built-in!

I transform from a mist to a bat and rip into the sack with my razor-sharp fangs. The material is super tough, so it takes a few bites before I tear a decent-sized hole.

And then a ghost flies out!

"Bram?" Aura says, looking around confused. "Is that you?"

I drop to the ground and go to kid-form.

"Shhh!" I whisper, putting my finger to my lips. "There are guards outside the door."

"Guards?" she whispers, looking at the bolted door.

"Where are we anyway? After I got sucked into that stupid vacuum bag I couldn't phase through it no matter what I tried. I don't know what that thing is made of."

"We're at DSI," I whisper. "They've created special weapons to capture monsters, including ghosts."

"DSI?" she asks. "What's that?"

Well, if Aura hasn't heard of them, then nobody has.

"I'll explain later," I whisper. "But we're in danger. We've got to find the others and get out of here as quickly as we can. Follow me."

But just as we start to move, we hear—

"B-Bram?"

Huh? Where's that voice coming from?

"Bram?" it repeats, sounding strangely familiar. "Are you here?"

"InvisiBill?" I whisper, looking around. "Is that you? Where are you?"

"Shackled to the table," he says.

Ah-ha. No wonder the table looked empty. And that's when I notice the shackles are closed. They must be locked around his wrists and ankles.

"The key is dangling off the side of the table," he says. "Ever-so-cruelly out of my reach."

"I've got you," I whisper. "But then again, maybe we're better off leaving you here."

"Not funny," InvisiBill whispers.

I use the key to get him free and now I've got two of my teammates back. Four more to go.

Six

"Listen," I say, "There are two other rooms to search and I'm guessing the others are split into pairs like you guys. This place is crawling with guards so you should wait here so you don't get caught."

"Get caught?" InvisiBill whispers. "She's a ghost and I'm invisible. Who's gonna catch us?"

"Dude," I whisper, "up until two seconds ago you were shackled to a table."

"Right," he says. "Sorry. Bad short-term memory."

"New plan," Aura says, "You said we needed to move fast so here's what we're gonna do. InvisiBill and I will take one room and you take the other. We'll be done twice as fast."

"That's not the plan," I say.

"Plans change," Aura says, folding her arms.

I stare into her blue eyes, reluctant to give in. I mean, she has no idea how brutal Agent M and DSI can be. But I also know she's not going to stay put.

"Fine," I say. "I'll search the room across the way and you do the one next door. But be careful. These guys are professional monster hunters and they can take you down easily. Uh-oh."

"What?" she whispers.

"The rest of the team aren't ghosts, mists, or invisible," I whisper. "How are we going to sneak them out of here?"

"We're not," she whispers. "A kid like Hairball is impossible to hide. After you get your group free, listen for my signal and we'll all rush the guards in the hall."

"Now there's a great plan," I whisper sarcastically.

"You got a better one?" she asks.

"Not really," I say.

"Then we'll see you in the hall," she says with a wink. "Come on, InvisiBill."

I roll my eyes as I go to mist-form. Even though Aura is as stubborn as an ox, I'm glad I found her first. No matter how tough the situation, she always finds a way to figure things out.

InvisiBill on the other hand…

This time I stay low, snaking my way across the hall, and when I enter my designated room I find two more of my friends imprisoned. Hairball is locked inside a cage like an animal while Stanphibian is chained beneath a giant heat lamp.

"Shhh!" I whisper, as I float next to Stanphibian and assume kid-form. His skin is all cracked and dried out.

"H-Help," Stanphibian stammers.

"I got you," I whisper.

Wow, this heat lamp is super-hot! Thank goodness he still has his fishbowl helmet on or he would have died from heat exhaustion. I quickly find the power switch and turn the lamp off, but the chain around his leg is too strong for me to break and I can't find the key.

"Thanks," he says, as I help him to his feet.

"Quiet," I whisper. "Let me free Hairball and he'll deal with your chain."

Six

But as I approach the cage, I find Hairball sitting cross-legged in the center, his fur sticking straight out all over his body.

"Careful," Hairball whispers. "The bars are electric."

"Clearly," I say. I look around until I find the key hanging on the wall. Then, I avoid the bars, pop the lock, and carefully open the door. "Can you bust Stan's chain? But do it quietly."

"No problem," Hairball whispers, and then he grabs Stanphibian's chain and breaks it off his leg without making a noise.

"Great job," I whisper.

"Thanks," Hairball says, casually tossing the chain over his shoulder.

"Hairball, no!" I whisper, but it's too late.

The chain CLANKS loudly on the cement floor.

"What's that?" comes a voice from outside.

"Seriously, Hairball?" I say.

"Sorry," Hairball says, cracking his knuckles. "Well, maybe you should stand back while I handle this."

Suddenly, the door swings open and a guard appears.

"Batter up!" Hairball yells.

And then he punches the man so hard he flies backward and breaks down the door across the hall. The next thing I know, I'm staring at Aura, Rage, and Kat through the broken down doorway!

"I thought I was giving the signal?" Aura says.

"Plans change," I say, shrugging my shoulders. "Let's

go!"

We rush into the hall and Hairball and Kat make short work of the remaining guards.

"This way!" I call out, leading the team around the corner and down a super long hallway.

"Do you know where you're going?" Aura asks.

"Nope," I say. "Just look for a way out."

"Hold on," Kat calls out. "I smell people up ahead. Lots of people. I think we should turn back. Like, now!"

We all skid to a stop, crashing into one another.

"Let's go back!" InvisiBill yells.

"We can't!" I say. "It's a dead-end!"

"Get them!" comes a woman's voice.

My heart races as I look down the hall to see an army of agents heading our way.

And leading the charge is Agent M!

"What now?" InvisiBill says.

I look around but there's nowhere to go. We're trapped in this hallway, unless…

"Hairball," I say. "Bust through that wall!"

"Got it," he says. And then he cocks back his giant fist and punches the wall. There's a massive BOOM but little else. "Ow!" he yells, shaking his hand.

Holy cow! There's barely a dent! What's that wall made of?

"We're doomed!" Rage says, breathing heavily.

"It's okay," I say, trying to sound calm even though I'm panicking inside. But the last thing we need is Rage flying off the handle.

But then again, maybe that's exactly what we need.

"Freeze!" Agent M orders.

"Rage!" I say, shaking his shoulders. "You've got to help us! You've got to become the beast!"

"W-What?" he says, looking at me confused.

"You need to become Monster Rage!" I say, shaking him harder. "You can easily bust through this wall. It's our only way out or we'll all die!"

"D-Die?" he says, his eyes getting bigger. "I-I don't want to die? B-But I can't control the monster."

"Dispose of them!" Agent M commands, her voice getting closer. "Except for the vampire! He's mine!"

"That's not true," I say. "You can control it. But we need you to do it now."

"N-Now?" he says.

"Yes," I say. "I know you can. When we were at Moreau's tower, I saw something different in you. I believe in you."

"They're closing in!" Aura yells. "Get ready!"

And when I look up I realize she's right. The agents have gotten a lot closer, and they're drawing their weapons!

"Rage!" I say.

But when I look back, his pupils have gone from blue to red. Holy cow! He's... doing it!

"Look out!" I warn the others.

Suddenly, Rage arches his back, and his entire body

expands! His shirt rips down the middle and his muscles balloon to ridiculous proportions! I back up, tripping over Hairball's leg. And when I look up, I'm staring at a seven-foot, purple monster with blond hair!

"What is that thing?" an agent yells.

"Who cares?" Agent M says. "Just kill it!"

Suddenly, bullets start flying and we duck behind Rage's huge body.

"RRRRAAAARRRRGGHHH!" Rage cries, as the bullets bounce off his chest and ricochet off the walls.

"Take it down!" Agent M orders. "Now!"

"Rage!" I call out. "Forget them! We need you to smash the wall! Get us out of here so we don't die!"

Rage looks down at me, his eyes seething with anger.

Uh-oh. I hope I didn't get this wrong.

"It's me, Bram!" I yell. "You can control this! I know you can!"

Suddenly, his eyebrows raise. Yes, he hears me!

"Now bust through this wall," I say. "Help us get out of here. Help us get to safety!"

"SSSAAAFFFEEETTTYYY!" Rage says.

And then he drives his powerful arms straight through the wall and pulls back a huge slab.

"Stop them!" Agent M yells. "They're getting away!"

But before the agents can get any closer, Rage lifts the massive chunk of wall over his head and throws it down the hallway, completely blocking their path.

"Let's go!" Aura says. "Everybody out!"

Six

The team streams through the hole, except for one.

"Rage!" I yell. "Let's go!"

"GGGRRRAAARRR!" Rage growls as he stares down the hall at our pursuers, his muscles twitching.

"Rage, no!" I say, stepping halfway through the opening to freedom. "You're part of our team! You're one of the Monstrosities! You belong with us!"

Rage looks at me and then back down the hall.

And then he comes thundering through the opening behind me.

D.S.I. CLASSIFIED PHOTOGRAPH

Rage Monster - Extremely Dangerous!!

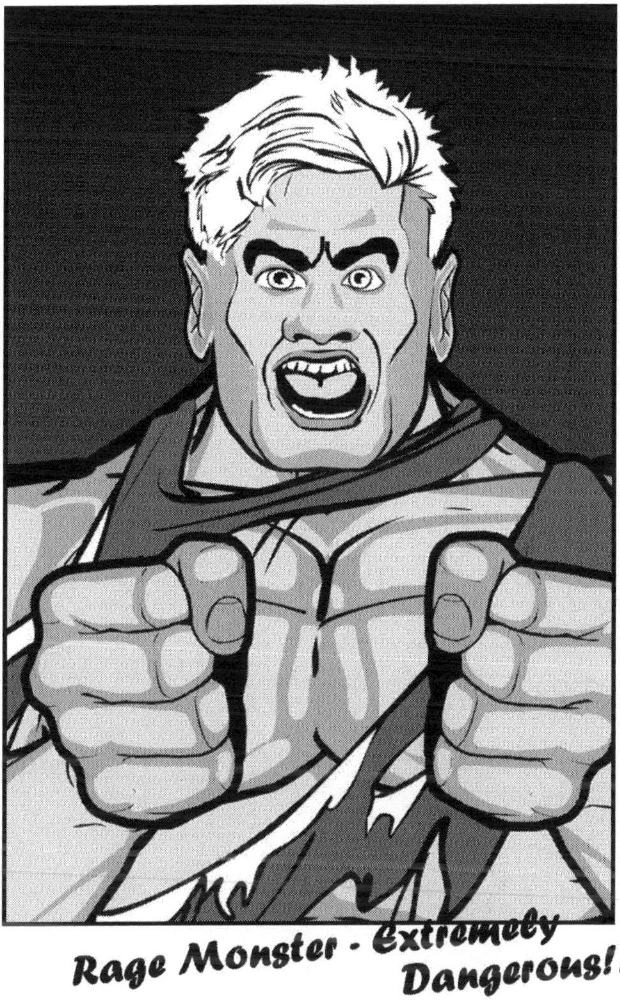

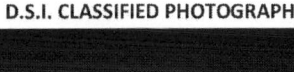

CHAPTER SEVEN

MONSTERS ON THE RUN

We're running for our lives.

As soon as we busted out of DSI headquarters we hit the nearby woods and took off. The problem is, DSI clearly doesn't want to let us go.

Somehow, we manage to dodge dozens of helicopters, tanks, and foot soldiers as we make our way through the underbrush. We've been lucky so far, but who knows how long that'll last. DSI is getting closer and closer but we can't give up.

Our lives are in the balance!

The only good news is Rage transformed back to a kid again. As soon as we got out of DSI, he took two lumbering steps before his eyes rolled back in his head and he passed out. Hairball is carrying Rage now but we need to make good on all of his hard work.

I'm so proud of him for mastering his monster side. He came through when we needed him most and now we need to get him—and all of us—to safety. I don't ever want to see the initials 'D.S.I.' again.

"Everybody down!" Aura whispers, and we huddle

beneath a large tree as a helicopter hovers overhead, its searchlight beaming through the branches.

"Stan, hide your head!" I whisper. "The light will reflect off your fishbowl."

Stanphibian burrows his noggin beneath Hairball's shaggy armpit, making me gag.

Seconds later the helicopter flutters away.

"That was close," InvisiBill says. "What do we do now?"

"Can someone tell me who's chasing us first?" Hairball asks. "I have no clue what's going on right now."

"They're called DSI," I say. "That's short for the Department of Supernatural Investigations, a secret government agency that protects the public from monsters. I met their leader, a woman named Agent M. She thinks we're working with Count Dracula and the Dark Ones."

"What?" Kat says. "That's ridiculous!"

"I agree," I say. "But she didn't believe me. She thinks all monsters are evil, so we must be evil too. And she was going to torture you unless I told her what she wanted to hear. Luckily, I escaped and now here we are."

"Wow," Hairball says. "How'd you manage to escape anyway? The rest of us were pretty well contained."

I open my mouth to answer but stop myself. For some reason, I'm hesitant to tell them about that strange, gray mist. I mean, first of all, I have no clue what it was. And secondly, they'll probably think I'm nuts.

"Who cares," InvisiBill says. "The important thing is he got out."

"True," Hairball says. "So, where do we go now?"

Seven

"Home," Aura says. "Back to school. We just need to figure out where we are right now. We need a map."

"No," Kat says, her whiskers bouncing as she sniffs the air. "We don't need a map. I think I can get us there."

"With just your schnoz?" Hairball asks

"Yep," Kat says, still sniffing. "Our school has a very distinct scent, and I think I've picked it up. It's faint, but it's there. Follow me but keep up because I don't want to lose the trail."

Then, she takes off, her tail flowing behind her.

"Great," InvisiBill says. "Now we're chasing a cat."

"Do you want to live?" Aura asks.

"Chasing now," InvisiBill says, as a pile of leaves kick up behind his feet.

As I follow the team, I think back to my conversation with Agent M. I still haven't told the team everything, and if Agent M is right we'll all have trouble adjusting to the real world once school ends. Sadly, I can kind of see what she's talking about. I mean, Van Helsing isn't teaching us anything about fitting into society. Our days are spent studying monster history and honing our monster abilities. We're not being taught anything about how to adapt to the real world after school is over.

If there even is an 'after.'

Now that Count Dracula is on the attack, society will look very different if we don't get our act together. And boy did we stumble out of the gate with this mission. If we keep this up, there's no way we'll stop Count Dracula.

Speaking of stopping Count Dracula, at some point I'm going to have to face him. Just the thought of being alone with him terrifies me. The fact that I nearly passed out when he was coming out of his coffin in my Survival Skills exam tells me I'm not ready.

And I'm not sure I ever will be.

"Take cover!" Kat whispers, snapping me back to reality. She's up ahead, waving for us to get down.

I stay low and make my way to her position. We've reached the end of the woods, and just up ahead is a small town—or rather, a small town in ruins.

It looks like a nuclear bomb went off. Plumes of black smoke rise into the sky, buildings are demolished, and vehicles are turned upside down. Yet, despite all of the destruction, there's an eerie silence.

And that's when I realize something.

There aren't any people.

"Look at that sign," Aura says, nodding to her left.

There's a bent, green highway sign leaning against a crushed dumpster bin. It reads:

WELCOME TO SMILEVILLE
POPULATION 3,575

"Smileville?" InvisiBill says. "I doubt anyone is smiling now."

"What happened to this place?" Hairball asks.

"I'm guessing the Dark Ones marched through here on their way to New York City," Aura says. "It's totally destroyed."

"Shhh!" Kat whispers, her ears pricking up. "I hear something coming."

"Wonderful," InvisiBill says.

I brace myself, but when I look back at the town, I

Seven

see a small, blond-haired girl with pigtails standing on the street corner. She's facing the other way, wearing a blue dress, and holding a teddy bear by the leg. She doesn't look older than six, and she's all alone.

"We've got to help her," I say, standing up. "She might be the only survivor!"

My instincts take over and I run out of the brush.

"Bram, wait!" I hear Aura yell.

But I can't wait. I mean, this poor girl's life has been wrecked because of me. Everything that's happened to her, everything that's happened to all of these innocent people, is all my fault.

I wish none of this ever happened.

I wish I wasn't the Blood Grail.

I wish I wasn't a vampire.

Running feels good right now. And even though I haven't eaten in a while, I crank on my super-speed to get to her as fast as I can. I couldn't forgive myself if something happened before I got there.

I mean, haven't I done enough?

But I have a decision to make. Do I just pick her up and keep running, scaring her half to death, or should I stop and talk her into coming with me? While a big part of me thinks scooping her up is the right thing to do, I figure the kid's been through enough trauma for one day.

I stop behind her and get down on one knee.

Better to connect at her level.

"Hey," I say gently, putting my hand on her shoulder. "I know you're probably scared right now, but why don't you come with me and my friends? I promise we'll take you to safety."

I smile, hoping to make her feel as comfortable as possible, but as she turns I recoil in horror. Because instead of talking to a sweet, wide-eyed little girl, I'm staring at a green, slack-jawed creature with red eyes, peeled skin, and rotting teeth!

I-I'm too late!

The little girl is… a zombie!

Suddenly, she grabs my hoodie!

Holy cow! If she bites me, I'll turn into a zombie too!

I push her away, but when I do her hand grips my hoodie tight and her arm detaches from her body!

I scream!

I yank her appendage from my hoodie when I realize it's still moving!

GROSS!

But as I throw the arm as far away as possible, I hear MOANING coming from both sides of me. That's when I see dozens of zombies lumbering my way, and even more are popping out all over town!

I'm totally outnumbered!

I start panicking, and then I remember I'm not alone.

I'm about to call for help, when—

POW!

"Dude," Hairball says, punching the lights out of three zombies with one blow. "Please don't run away all bat-crazy again."

"Yeah," Stanphibian adds, picking up one zombie and throwing it at a group of others.

Seconds later, the other Monstrosities join in and we're quickly in the middle of a monster battle royale! Aura stands guard over a still-unconscious Rage while the

Seven

rest of us do everything we can to keep the zombies away. But no matter how many we knock down, more just keep showing up!

"There's too many of them!" Kat yells as she kicks a zombie right between the eyes.

She's right! Hundreds of zombies are swarming our way! I could turn into a bat and save myself, but other than Aura, the rest of the team would be overwhelmed. I could never leave them behind, but how can I get us out of this mess?

Just then, a ten-foot wall of fire flares up in my face and I jump back! Where'd that come from? But then I realize the flames aren't just in front of me, they're circling the whole team, separating us from the zombie onslaught!

But strangely, there's no heat.

And that's when I realize what's happening.

We're being rescued!

"Get back you vile creatures!" comes a familiar voice.

It's Hexum!

The flames grow larger and the zombies back away in fear. Then, a pair of hairy, spider legs wrap around my body and lift me into the air. Seconds later, I'm face-to-face with Crawler.

"Thanks!" I say. "But grab Rage next. He needs the most help."

"On it," Crawler says.

A minute later, he's leg-lifted the rest of the team to safety. Once Aura floats over, Hexum erects a massive fire barrier behind us and we head for Crawler's jeep.

"How did you find us?" Aura asks.

"Actually, by tracking you," Crawler says, holding up his arm to reveal a familiar-looking Spirit Sensor around his wrist. "Professor Morris still has it programmed to read your ghost-signal. He never reprogrammed it, and based on how often we need to track you guys down, he probably never will. What happened to Rage?"

"He saved us by turning into the monster," I say. "But then he passed out."

"Really?" Crawler says, placing Rage gently in the jeep. "Well, we nearly passed out when we got back from New York City and discovered you were gone."

"Enough small talk," Hexum barks. "Everyone in the jeep. Now!"

Uh-oh. Hexum is clearly agitated.

As I hop inside, Hairball and Stanphibian squeeze in beside me, but honestly, their stink is the last thing on my mind. I'm thrilled Crawler and Hexum saved us, but I suspect whatever we've just been through will pale in comparison to what Van Helsing has in store for us.

Crawler turns on the engine, and as we hit the road I look back at the absolute disaster we've left behind. No matter what I do, I can't shake that little girl's zombie face from my mind.

"My, what a lovely drive," InvisiBill says, breaking the awkward silence. "So, does anybody have any plans for the weekend? I know I'm—"

"Quiet!" Hexum orders, holding his forehead. "I simply do not have the mental capacity for your senseless drivel. Now please, do not utter another word for the rest of the trip."

"Right," InvisiBill says. Then, I get a whiff of his bad

breath as he leans across Hairball and whispers, "In case you need a translation, that means we're in really big trouble."

CHAPTER EIGHT

AN UNEXPECTED GUEST

Van Helsing is not a happy camper.

I could tell from the second we walked into his office that this was going to be ugly. Unfortunately, we'll have to wait until we finish explaining ourselves to see how ugly. But at least we have a plan this time.

Before we entered Van Helsing's office we agreed that Aura and I would do all of the talking. Everyone else would stay quiet, especially InvisiBill. The only one lucky enough to be spared from this ordeal is Rage since Crawler took him to the infirmary.

Aura kicks things off, and I have to say, she's doing a great job. The way she's explaining it, we had no choice but to investigate that cargo ship. In her words, we were 'morally obligated' to defy Van Helsing's orders once we found out about Count Dracula's ship. Anything less would have been irresponsible.

By the time it's my turn I'm pumped up. I pick up right where she left off, covering our discovery of the dirt boxes, being captured by DSI, and our escape from their

Eight

death trap. I end things by stating the obvious, we were just at the right place at the wrong time.

Then, I nod and flash a big smile. I feel pretty good about what I told them. But I didn't tell them everything.

For one, I left out what Agent M said about Van Helsing. I mean, why poke the bear? Oh, and I also left out the part about the mysterious gray mist. I'll mention that later. Like, after we're out of hot water.

Once I wrap up, I expect loads of questions from Van Helsing and Hexum, but instead, all I get is silence. Long, awkward, uncomfortable silence. I swallow hard and shift my gaze from Van Helsing's penetrating stare.

After a while, I'm sweating. And then—

"I know you think your actions are justified," Van Helsing says, "but you do not realize how fortunate you are not to be dead—or worse, undead."

His words strike me funny. I mean, it never dawned on me that we could have ended up as part of Count Dracula's undead army. The thought of a Hairball-zombie or Stanphibian-zombie makes me shiver.

"If we are operating from a place of 'moral obligation,'" he continues, "then as Headmaster, it is my moral obligation to provide you with the consequences of your actions."

I glance at Hexum who's sporting a sly smile. I bet he's loving this. My pain is his joy.

Then, I jump as a hand lands on my shoulder.

"Get ready," InvisiBill mutters under his breath.

I shrug him off and brace myself. Given the magnitude of what we've done, I'm expecting Van Helsing to nail us this time. If this isn't the last straw then I don't know what is. It wouldn't surprise me if he expelled the whole lot of us.

Aura and I meet eyes and I take a deep breath.

"Therefore," Van Helsing says, "I have decided that you have suffered enough for your actions."

"What?" Hexum and InvisiBill blurt out simultaneously.

"Your continued disobedience is a signal I can no longer ignore," Van Helsing says. "You have demonstrated that you are eager and ready to join this fight, and I will no longer stand in your way."

There's a collective gasp.

"Wait," Hairball says. "Are you serious?"

"Yes," Van Helsing says. "The horrors of New York City and Smileville will be the reality across the globe unless we stop Count Dracula once and for all."

As he utters those words I can't help but notice he's staring at me.

"From this point forward," Van Helsing continues, "you will no longer be students, but soldiers. Your primary duty as soldiers is to prepare yourselves, both physically and mentally, for the difficult road ahead. Because once you receive the call to battle you must answer. Are those consequences satisfactory?"

"Oh, yeah!" Hairball says, pumping his fist. "We

Eight

finally get to fight!"

"Hold on," InvisiBill says. "Does that mean our exams don't count?"

"That is correct," Van Helsing says.

"Woohoo!" InvisiBill screams, right in my ear.

"Now I suggest you get to work," Van Helsing says. "Your time will come sooner than you think. You are all dismissed. Except for you, Bram. I would like to speak with you further."

Great.

All of my excitement fades as I watch the team high fiving one another as they exit. Then, I notice one person who isn't celebrating with the others. It's Aura, and she shoots me a worried look before floating away.

"Professor Hexum," Van Helsing says. "You are also dismissed."

"Yes, Headmaster," he says and then glares at me before he exits.

Well, so much for his exam. I guess I'll never know the full extent of what he had planned for me.

"Bram," Van Helsing says, rising from his chair. "Walk with me."

"Um, okay," I say.

That's strange, he's never asked me to walk with him before, but I follow him out of his cluttered office. Even though my friends are long gone, I can still hear InvisiBill whooping it up in the distance. Van Helsing walks slowly down the hallway with his hands clasped behind his back.

I'm not sure what he wants to talk to me about, but I'm guessing it's not good. We walk silently for a while, making our way through the building into the grand entrance hall. It's late, so no kids are rushing to make their classes before the bell goes off.

Finally, as we cross to the wing on the other side, Van Helsing says—

"Tell me more about your conversation with Agent M. We have quite a history together."

I look at him surprised. Well, I wasn't expecting that. I mean, I didn't think he knew who she was. But as I start to open my mouth, I debate if I should tell him what she said about the kids who graduate from here. But now that we're alone I figure I might as well go for it.

"Um, there's not much to tell," I say, nervously. "Except that, well, she did mention she's rounded up lots of monsters who graduated from here. She said they don't fit into the real world and become menaces to society."

"I see," Van Helsing says, raising a bushy eyebrow. "And do you believe her?"

"D-Do I believe her?" I stammer. "Well, I mean..."

"Did she tell you how many monsters DSI has captured?"

"No," I say. "I-I don't think she told me that."

"Interesting," Van Helsing says. "Bram, do you know how many students have graduated from our academy?"

"Um, no," I say.

Eight

"One thousand, five hundred, and twenty-seven," Van Helsing says. "And do you know how many of our graduates have been captured by DSI?"

"No," I say.

"Three," Van Helsing says. "That is far less than one percent. The rest of DSI's victims never attended our school."

"Really?" I say.

"Really," Van Helsing says, looking me in the eyes. "You could say DSI is one of the reasons I founded this school in the first place. It is my life's mission to provide a sanctuary for Supernatural children. Here they can learn to control their gifts without fearing for their lives. Here they can avoid persecution at the hands of monster-hunting organizations like DSI. I have known of Agent M for many years and she is not to be trusted."

Wow. Well, I guess I was wrong to believe her. But why would she tell me that stuff in the first place? Maybe she was trying to get me to spill information?

"But we have more to fear than DSI," Van Helsing continues. "We must stop Count Dracula before it is too late. And our task will only get more difficult."

"What's that supposed to mean?" I ask.

"Follow me," he says, leading me down a hallway I've never stepped foot in before. A sign on the wall reads:

FACULTY LOUNGE

Hmmm, maybe he's taking me for a late-night snack? But as we approach the double doors to the kitchen he walks right by. Disappointed, I look through the window and see Professor Seward eating a sandwich. My stomach grumbles loudly but Van Helsing ignores it and leads me to the end of the hallway, stopping in front of an old grandfather clock.

I have no clue what we're doing here. I mean, it's a nice clock and all, made of mahogany and standing several feet taller than Van Helsing, but if he needed to know the time we passed a million other clocks on the way over here.

"Um, are we waiting here for a reason?" I ask.

"We have an appointment," Van Helsing says.

"We do?" I say.

"Indeed," he says. "In approximately one minute."

One minute? I look at the clock and notice it's 11:59 p.m. I follow the second hand as it ticks around the face of the clock until it finally strikes midnight.

There's a loud DONG, and suddenly, the front panels of the clock open wide revealing a long hallway! I lean forward to take a closer look and do a double take. Nope, I'm definitely not seeing things. There's actually a hallway inside this clock!

"Follow me," Van Helsing says, stepping inside.

"You mean, inside the clock?" I ask, my mind still refusing to believe there's an actual hallway inside a clock.

"Yes," Van Helsing says. "You will be safe."

Eight

"Um, okay," I say, bending down and stepping cautiously inside. But as I straighten up, I look around in disbelief at the mahogany hallway.

"It takes some getting used to," Van Helsing says. "We call it a 'pocket clock.' Professor Holmwood discovered it on one of her many adventures. At the time it was being used to store biscuits, but we use it to hold 'other' things.'"

Other things? Like what?

But I soon get my answer, because as we reach the end of the hallway there's a prison cell! And sitting inside is a blindfolded man!

At first, I'm taken aback. I mean, this was the last thing I was expecting. But as I study his face more closely I realize I know this man!

"Dr. Renfield!" I exclaim.

Suddenly, my heart starts racing. The last time I saw him, he hypnotized and manipulated me. But before we could do anything about it he escaped.

"Mr. Murray?" Dr. Renfield says, perking up. "Is that you? What a surprise. How have you been?"

"What's he doing here?" I ask Van Helsing. "And why is he blindfolded?"

"He is my guest," Van Helsing says. "And if you will allow, I will answer your second question momentarily."

"Where did you find him?" I ask.

"In New York City," Van Helsing says. "One of Crawler's scouts reported that he was in the area. But do not worry, he cannot escape and he cannot lie. Professor Morris put him under the influence of a truth serum."

A truth serum?

"Tell us, Renfield," Van Helsing says. "Do you have anything you would like to say to Mr. Murray?"

"Why, yes," Dr. Renfield says, standing up. "I am so sorry for controlling you against your will. But I hope you understand it was not my choice. You see, at times I am not in control of my own mind."

"Huh?" I say. "What does that mean?"

"Go ahead, Renfield," Van Helsing says. "Show him."

"Show me?" I say. "Show me what?"

Then, Dr. Renfield reaches for his neck and rolls down the fabric of his black, turtleneck shirt, revealing two pink puncture marks.

Holy cow! That's a legit vampire bite!

"It is Count Dracula's signature," Van Helsing says. "The vampire bite itself does not always result in death. Sometimes it has another purpose, as blood contact forges an unbreakable mental bond between Count Dracula and his victim, providing Count Dracula great influence over the victim's mind. This is what happened to Dr. Renfield, and that also answers your other question. We blindfolded Dr. Renfield so he cannot share what he sees with Count Dracula."

Hold on a second. If Count Dracula can form a mental bond just by drinking blood, then maybe that's why I hear him in my head sometimes. I mean, the blood

Eight

coursing through Count Dracula's veins comes from my body! That's crazy scary.

And speaking of crazy scary...

"But isn't it dangerous even having him here?" I ask. "Won't he give our plans away to Count Dracula?"

"Thanks to the truth serum, Dr. Renfield will inform us if Count Dracula reaches out to him," Van Helsing says. "Thus far, there has been no contact. However, also thanks to the truth serum, Dr. Renfield has been very helpful in sharing Count Dracula's plans with us. Renfield, would you mind sharing Count Dracula's plans with Mr. Murray?"

"Certainly," Dr. Renfield says. "While Count Dracula's primary objective is to rule over mankind, it is not his only goal. You see, despite all of his power, his biggest fear is true death. And with the existence of another vampire who could destroy him once and for all, Count Dracula wants to ensure that he lives forever. Therefore, he has tasked the Dark Ones with finding the one artifact that could resurrect his body and spirit, even if he is destroyed by another vampire."

Dr. Renfield's words make me shudder.

Resurrect? As in, come back to life?

"W-What artifact does that?" I ask.

"It is called the Crown of Souls," Dr. Renfield says.

The Crown of Souls?

I've never even heard of it.

But before I can ask about it, Van Helsing stops me

by putting his hand on my arm and his finger to his lips.

"Thank you, Renfield," Van Helsing says. "That will be all for now. Good night."

Then, Van Helsing nods at me to follow him out.

"Good night?" Renfield says, pressing against the cell bars and shouting after us. "Van Helsing, wait! Won't you release me? I promise I won't hurt anyone! Mr. Murray? Please, release me! Mr. Murray?"

But Van Helsing doesn't stop. I hate hearing Dr. Renfield's cries of desperation, but it's not like he can be trusted. Especially if Count Dracula has so much influence over him.

When we're well out of earshot, Van Helsing says—

"I hope that was not too disturbing for you?"

"A little," I say. "But I don't understand. What is the Crown of Souls?"

"It is a Supernatural artifact with tremendous power," Van Helsing says. "According to legend, if you are wearing the Crown of Souls when you are slain, it will resurrect your body and spirit, even if you are a vampire."

"So, wait a minute," I say. "Are you saying that even if I destroy Count Dracula, if he's wearing this Crown of Souls thing he'll come back to life again?"

"Precisely," Van Helsing says.

My stomach drops. I mean, let's say I do somehow manage to destroy him—and I don't even know how that could happen—the thought of him coming back to life is absolutely terrifying. All of that effort would be for

Eight

nothing!

"Then, we can't let him get it!" I say.

"I agree," Van Helsing says. "I did not want us to discuss it openly in front of Dr. Renfield, but we must recover the Crown of Souls before Count Dracula does."

"Wait," I say, stopping short. "Did you say 'we.'"

"I did," Van Helsing says. "I suggest you get some rest. I have some preparation to do and then we will depart in a few hours. Oh, and there is one more thing. You must tell no one."

I feel my eyebrows rising with surprise as I take in what Van Helsing just said. I mean, why is he asking me not to tell anyone about something so important?

"Um, sure," I say. "But why not?"

"The Dark Ones have many secret operatives," Van Helsing says. "We simply cannot risk the possibility of anyone revealing our whereabouts. Do you understand?"

"Yeah," I say. "I understand."

"Very good," he says. "Rest up. We will regroup shortly."

CLASSIFIED

Person(s) of Interest

CODE NAME: NONE

REAL NAME: LAWRENCE SEWARD

BASE OF OPERATIONS: VAN HELSING ACADEMY

FACTS: Lawrence Seward is the tenured professor of Supernatural History at the Van Helsing Academy. He is also a notable archeologist specializing in the identification and recovery of supernatural artifacts. He is a trusted advisor of Lothar Van Helsing.

Category: Natural
Sub-Type: None
Height: 6'0"
Weight: 285 lbs

FIELD OBSERVATIONS:

- Highly observant
- Travels often for archeological fieldwork
- Is deceptively quick on his feet
- Is armed at all times so approach with caution

STATUS: ACTIVE TARGET

DEPARTMENT OF SUPERNATURAL INVESTIGATIONS

CHAPTER NINE

TOO LITTLE TOO LATE

I open the door to find a ghost in my room.

"Aura?" I say. "What are you doing here?"

"We need to talk," she says.

She's sitting on the edge of Rage's bed with her arms crossed, which is never a good sign. Rage, of course, is still in the infirmary.

"Um, okay," I say, entering the room and closing the door behind me. I take off my hoodie and notice there's a giant hole in the right pocket. "Great. This must be from that zombie girl. Well, it's not like I didn't deserve it."

"What do you mean?" Aura asks.

"I mean this whole nightmare is my fault," I say, sitting on my bed and poking my finger through the hole. "If I never got captured by Faustius, Count Dracula would still be a spirit instead of the flesh-and-blood monster he is today. And then everyone's lives would be normal."

I toss the hoodie on my desk chair.

"Your fault?" Aura says, her eyebrows raised. "Bram,

this isn't your fault. If anything, it's my fault. The only reason you were in Faustius' lair was because of me, remember? My stupid curiosity has gotten us into more trouble than we can count. So, if we're going to go down that road you should blame me for everything."

"What?" I say. "That's ridiculous. I would never do that. It's not your fault."

"Okay," she says, "then it's not yours either."

We stare at each other for a while.

"Look," Aura says finally breaking the silence, "wallowing in self-pity won't change the past. All we can do now is save the future."

She's right about that, but the question is how? Saving the future is going to be difficult, especially if Count Dracula gets the Crown of Souls. But Van Helsing had me swear not to tell anyone about that. Time to change the subject.

"So," I say half-smiling. "Is that what you came to tell me, oh wise one?"

"No," she says. "I wanted to talk about what happened in Van Helsing's office. We're not ready."

"Ready?" I ask. "Ready for what?"

"To fight," she says, standing up. "To be soldiers. To take on Count Dracula and the Dark Ones. Do you honestly think Hairball and Stanphibian are ready to fight hordes of evil monsters? And what about Rage who can barely control himself? Or InvisiBill who can't follow simple directions? Or Kat who just got here and hasn't

Nine

even been properly trained? If they go into battle they'll be slaughtered. Something is wrong with Van Helsing."

"What?" I say, surprised. "What do you mean?"

"I mean he's off his rocker," Aura says. "I get it that the war has started, but until today he would never put innocent kids on the front lines. Someone needs to talk to him about it, and I think that someone is you?"

"Me?" I say.

"Yes, you," she says. "You have a special relationship with him. He talks to you all the time. Maybe you can tell him we're not ready to be soldiers? Maybe you can get him to change his mind?"

The concern in her blue eyes tugs at my heartstrings, but I seriously doubt I can convince Van Helsing of anything. But I know she's right. If Crawler and Hexum hadn't shown up in Smileville we would have been overrun by zombies.

"Okay, okay," I say. "I'll talk to him. But he might not listen."

"Thank you, Bram!" she says.

And before I can respond, she leans over and gives me a big hug, but her arms go right through my body, sending chills down my spine.

"Sorry," she says, pulling back awkwardly.

"N-No," I say. "It's okay. Really."

She smiles nervously, her arms behind her back. Boy, if ghosts could blush her cheeks would be fire engine red.

"So, um, what did Van Helsing say after we left?" she

asks, quickly changing the subject.

Uh-oh. What am I going to tell her? I don't want to lie to her, but I have to stick to what I promised Van Helsing.

"Bram?" she asks. "Are you okay?"

"What? Yeah," I say. "He just wanted some more info about Agent M and DSI. So, I filled him in on some of those details."

There, that wasn't a lie.

"Oh, okay," she says. "Speaking of more info, I'm still trying to track down the cargo that arrived on that first ship from Romania."

"Really?" I say. "Um, here's a newsflash, but didn't you just tell me your curiosity has gotten us into more trouble than we can count?"

"Good point," she says, "but I know there's something there. I mean, why is Count Dracula shipping dirt from Romania to America? And according to those sailors you overheard, this was the second shipment. So, where did that first shipment go after it got here?"

"Great question," I say. "No clue."

"Exactly," she says, with a suspicious look in her eyes. "It's a mystery, and I love a good mystery."

"Then maybe you should stick to detective novels," I say. "They'll be less dangerous for everyone."

"Ha," she says. "Anyway, I've got things to do. Thanks for, well, listening to me. And thanks for talking to Van Helsing."

Nine

"Yeah," I say. "No problem."

"Have a good night," she says, and then phases through my door.

I kick off my shoes and lie down on my bed.

Well, I know I'll be seeing Van Helsing later, but I'm pretty sure I won't be having a good night.

***

After my talk with Aura, my stomach reminds me I'm starving! I put my shoes and hoodie back on and head down to the cafeteria. I know it's not open at this hour, but luckily I find some imps playing dice games out back and they let me in.

I raid the pantry, gobbling down anything red I can find while politely declining anything the imps offer me. After all, now isn't the time for unnecessary risks. When I'm finished I thank them and head back to my room.

And then I wait.

Crawler comes for me an hour later.

"Ready?" he asks.

"I guess so," I say, standing up.

We meet up with Van Helsing and Hexum at the garage. Barely a word is spoken as we load into Crawler's jeep and take off. Van Helsing and I are sitting in the back, giving me the perfect opportunity to have that conversation I promised Aura. But for some reason, now doesn't seem like the right time.

Van Helsing is staring out the window, and I can only imagine what he's thinking. I mean, this is a major mission. He's probably running through millions of scenarios about how we'll get the Crown of Souls before Count Dracula.

But then I notice his eyes are closed.

I lean forward and take a closer look when I realize he's sleeping. That's funny, I've never actually seen Van Helsing sleep before. I guess he has our plan all set.

Well, I don't know how long it will take to get to wherever we're going, and I'm actually feeling sleepy myself. So, I close my eyes and drift off.

***

"Bram," comes a voice. "It is time."

Huh?

I open my eyes, and for a split second, I have no idea where I am. I look out the window and see trees and mountains, and when I look the other way I see Van Helsing staring at me.

"We have arrived," he says. "It is time."

"Right," I say, rubbing my eyes.

Van Helsing steps out of the jeep and reaches back inside, pulling out a black crossbow. Something's off but I don't know what. Then, it hits me.

What's he doing with a black crossbow? Normally, he has the Crossbow of Purity, which is silver.

Nine

"Headmaster?" I say. "What happened to the Crossbow of Purity?"

"Oh, it is broken," he says. "But this one is a worthy substitute."

Um, okay. I didn't even know the Crossbow of Purity could break. I step out of the jeep and a chilly breeze makes me shiver. I pull my hood over my head and take a look around. We're parked on a dirt road that ends at the base of a sweeping mountain range.

"Where are we?" I ask.

"According to my research," Van Helsing says, "the Crown of Souls should be located here."

"You mean, up in the mountains?" I ask.

"No," Van Helsing says, loading a bolt into his crossbow, "down inside the cavern."

I swallow hard. Did he just say 'cavern?'

Why do I have a bad feeling about this?

"Let's go," Crawler says.

I follow the three men as they make their way across the rocky terrain towards the largest mountain. At first, my eyes can't help but drift up to the mountain's soaring peak. But as we climb over a ridge, I spot an ominous cave burrowing deep into the mountain itself.

Two dark, slanted stones protrude above the entrance like watchful eyes, while jagged rocks hang into the opening like sharp fangs. If I didn't know better, I'd say we were walking straight into the mouth of a monster!

Van Helsing gathers us outside the cave.

"The artifact we seek should be inside," Van Helsing says.

"Should be?" Hexum says. "What does that mean?"

"It means the research has led us here, but we may be in the wrong place," Van Helsing says.

"To that point," Crawler says, "it's also a cavern. So, don't be surprised if there are bats in there."

"Bats?" I say, my voice cracking nervously.

They all look at me funny and I feel embarrassed.

"Um, sorry," I say quickly. "I mean, I love bats."

"According to my records," Van Helsing says, "the cavern will descend gradually for three hundred feet before opening into a large chamber. The Crown of Souls should be inside that chamber, but that is not all. According to legend, the artifact is protected by a guardian."

"A guardian?" Crawler says. "What kind of guardian?"

"A mummy," Van Helsing says. "Supposedly, it will come to life if anyone attempts to steal the Crown of Souls."

A mummy? Seriously?

"Got it," Crawler whispers, his voice not wavering in the least. "Let's get this show on the road."

Crawler and Hexum head for the cave entrance, but for some reason, my feet don't want to move.

"Come, Bram," Van Helsing says. "Do not worry, I will be right behind you."

Nine

"Right," I say, trying to look brave.

I fall in line behind Hexum, and Van Helsing brings up the rear. The cave is cold so I pull my hands into my sleeves to keep them warm. I can see clearly in the dark, but the others need flashlights, and the rock walls sparkle as they shine their lights around.

Strangely, for a guy who can transform into a bat, I've never actually been in a cavern before. I have to say, it's pretty incredible. With the dripstone formations and reflective pools of water, it feels like you're walking on another planet. The ever-changing landscape, from ten-foot stalactites to thirty-foot stalagmites, is truly amazing.

One day I'd love to bring the team down here but under entirely different circumstances.

SKREEEE!

"Get down!" Crawler whispers.

I duck just as a colony of bats zooms over our heads. Holy cow! There must be hundreds of them! I stay low until the last one clears, my heart pumping fast. That was close, but then I realize something.

We've lost the element of surprise.

"Come on," Crawler whispers.

As we continue, I remember my conversation with Aura. She's right, maybe none of us are ready for this, including me. I mean, I have no idea why I'm even here. Van Helsing has never included me on his missions before, so why did he rope me into this one? I'm pretty sure they could have handled it without me. I'd love to ask him about it but it's kind of late now.

"Up here," Crawler whispers, waving us ahead.

And when we reach his position, we're standing on a rocky ledge looking into a circular chamber with a high ceiling and multiple levels, each with its own tunnel. And there, sitting in the center of the floor is a gray tomb!

That's it!

The Crown of Souls must be in there!

"Let's go," Crawler says, using his spider legs to gracefully climb down a crude rock stairway.

We follow him far less gracefully, congregating around the dusty, stone tomb. As I study it, it's hard not to notice its large size, perfect for holding a kid-eating mummy.

"Open it," Hexum says to Crawler. "But slowly."

Crawler nods and slides his spider legs beneath the lid. Well, if there's really a mummy in there then I'm probably standing a little too close. But when I step back I nearly jump out of my skin as a hand clamps down on my shoulder.

"Stay right here," Van Helsing orders.

Um, okay. What's wrong with him?

But as Crawler lifts the lid, the tomb is empty!

There's no mummy inside, and more importantly, no Crown of Souls!

"What foul trick is this?" Hexum says, looking at me and Van Helsing.

But then his eyes go wide.

Nine

And when I glance over, I see Van Helsing's crossbow pointed right at Hexum's chest!

"I'd say a good one," Van Helsing says.

HA! HA! HA!

Maniacal laughter echoes through the chamber, and suddenly, four werewolves pop out of the tunnels above!

"Well done, 'Headmaster,'" comes a familiar, evil voice from somewhere up high. "Well done indeed."

And that's when I see him, standing on the highest ledge with a round, wooden object in his hand.

It's Count Dracula!

And he's got the Crown of Souls!

CHAPTER TEN

BAD BLOOD

I'm floored right now.

I mean, in the blink of an eye everything just went bonkers! Count Dracula has the Crown of Souls, we're surrounded by werewolves, and Van Helsing is pointing his crossbow right at Hexum's chest!

I don't know what's going on, and Van Helsing is gripping my shoulder so tight I can't pull away!

"Headmaster," Crawler says, "are you okay? You do realize you're pointing your crossbow at Professor Hexum, right?"

"I know where my crossbow is pointed," Van Helsing says. "And I am perfectly fine, thank you very much."

"Yes, he is perfect isn't he?" Count Dracula says from high on his ledge. "Nearly perfect in every way."

"What are you talking about?" Crawler says.

"I know exactly what he is talking about," Hexum says, staring into Van Helsing's eyes. "You aren't Van Helsing, are you?"

"No," Van Helsing says, flashing an evil grin. "Not

Ten

exactly."

Huh? What's going on?

Suddenly, I feel something strange spreading across my shoulder, and when I look over Van Helsing's fingers aren't fingers, but flesh-colored tendrils expanding down my hoodie! And when I look up I don't see Van Helsing anymore, but a creature with a distorted head and folds of skin shifting across his face!

"A doppelganger!" Hexum says.

A… doppelganger? Suddenly, I remember Professor Holmwood talking about doppelgangers in our Monsterology class. They're shapeshifters who can duplicate the physical and vocal characteristics of someone else! And they're pure evil!

"Indeed," the doppelganger says. "But I'm no ordinary doppelganger."

Suddenly, everything clicks into place. No wonder Aura thought Van Helsing was off his rocker. It was never Van Helsing at all!

But wait a second, how could a doppelganger even step foot on campus? I mean, the Artifacts of Virtue are supposed to protect the school from evil.

"I'm known as a doppelganger-superior," the creature continues. "The best mercenary-for-hire around. Unlike my weaker kin, with a simple touch, I not only mimic the surface characteristics of my victims but their thoughts and desires as well. As long as I stay in character, I'm as good as the real thing."

"So," I say, "you weren't the real Van Helsing when we talked to Dr. Renfield?"

"Nope," the doppelganger-superior says. "I've been pretending to be your sappy headmaster since New York City. I knew you and your 'mentor' had a rocky relationship, so bringing you to see Renfield was a simple ploy to earn your trust. And that's how I got you here without you suspecting a thing."

As his words sink in, I feel like such a fool.

"It was a trap from the start," Hexum says, disgusted. "Congratulations on fooling us and the Artifacts of Virtue. Now, where is the real Van Helsing?"

"Do not worry about your beloved Headmaster," Count Dracula says, floating down to ground level, his cape billowing behind him. "He is in good hands. Rest assured that he is enjoying his 'special' accommodations."

Seeing Count Dracula up close shocks me. Somehow, he looks even younger than when I saw him last at Dr. Moreau's tower. His cheeks are fuller, and I can see his muscular shoulders through his cape. It's like he's aging backward, which can only mean one thing.

He must be drinking human blood again.

"Wait until I get my legs on you," Crawler says, stepping towards Count Dracula, but the four werewolves jump down to block his path.

"Crawler, wait," Hexum says, putting his arm out. Then, he looks at the Crown of Souls in Count Dracula's hand and says, "You have what you want, now let us go."

Ten

"I do," Count Dracula says, putting the artifact on his head. "But this is not the only thing I came for."

For the first time, I get a good look at the Crown of Souls, a collection of intertwining twigs woven into a circular crown. All I know is that if I destroy Count Dracula while he's wearing it, he'll come back to life. And that's not a good thing.

"What do you want?" Hexum asks.

"Is it not obvious?" Count Dracula says, turning towards me. "I want the boy."

What? I try pulling away, but the doppelganger-superior still has me in his powerful grasp.

"Retrieving the Crown of Souls before you was easy," Count Dracula says. "But getting you to deliver the child was far more difficult. Fortunately, I have plenty of operatives at my disposal."

"I just want my pay," the doppelganger-superior says.

"And you will receive it," Count Dracula says.

"I assume your list of operatives includes Renfield?" Hexum says. "I must admit, you used him perfectly to set your trap. I thought it was an odd coincidence to find him in New York City where you also unleashed your attack, but now it makes sense. Well played, but unfortunately, the child is not yours for the taking."

"And who will stop me?" Count Dracula says.

Hexum opens his mouth but thinks better of it.

I look at Count Dracula and shudder. I can't believe it. All of this trickery was to get me here. Now I know why Van Helsing invited me on this mission. It was all to bring me to Count Dracula!

"Hello, Bram," Count Dracula says. "Have you reconsidered my offer?"

"Your offer?" I repeat. "You mean, the one to join you and rule the world?"

"Yes," he says. "Why should we fight and risk one of us dying? After all, we are the last of our kind. The last of a magnificent and superior race feared and envied by all of humankind. Imagine how much I could teach you. Envision how we could rule together. I, the King of Darkness, and you, the Prince of Darkness."

As his lips curl into a menacing smile I feel disgusted. I mean, I'm not evil. I don't want to be a bloodsucking vampire like him. I'll do anything to stop myself from getting to that point. And I mean anything.

"Open your pointy ears," I say, "because I want you to get this through your thick skull. I will NEVER, EVER join you! Got it?"

"That is a shame," Count Dracula says, his smile fading. "Because that means I have no use for you." And then he opens his mouth wide, revealing razor-sharp fangs!

"Bram, go!" Crawler yells. He tries pushing past the werewolves but they wrestle him to the ground.

I try to run, but the stupid doppelganger-superior still has me by the shoulder! I'm about to mist, when—

RRRAAUURRRGGGHHH!

Ten

Everyone freezes.

What's that noise?

Just then, the tomb's lid CLANGS onto the floor and two bony hands emerge from inside, gripping the sides.

"What?" Count Dracula says, turning.

Suddenly, a bandaged figure with dried-out skin, cracked lips, and yellow eyes leaps out of the tomb and attacks Count Dracula!

I can't believe it! It's… the mummy!

And it's trying to take back the Crown of Souls!

"Get him off me you fools!" Count Dracula yells, holding the mummy's wrists.

The werewolves release Crawler to help their master, but the mummy is too strong. As they tussle on the ground, Hexum shoots Crawler a look, and the spider-man nods back.

"But that's impossible," the doppelganger-superior mutters, watching the action. "It can't be real. I made up the story about the mummy just for fun."

"Shoot it, you imbecile!" Count Dracula yells, as he finally flips the mummy over his head into the rock wall.

The doppelganger-superior finally lets me go and aims his crossbow at the mummy.

THWIP!

The arrow pierces the mummy's chest, knocking it down for a moment. But then it gets back up.

"Time to leave," Crawler says, grabbing me with his spider legs and throwing me over his shoulder like a sack of potatoes. "This is our chance."

"But the Crown of Souls?" I say. "We can't just let Count Dracula have—"

"It's too late, kid," Crawler says, cutting me off. "We need to get you out alive."

"But what about Hexum?" I say.

"I am behind you, Mr. Murray," Hexum calls out.

As Crawler scales the stairs with ease, I see Hexum behind us, struggling to make his way up the rocky incline.

"Stop!" a voice echoes through the chamber.

But this time it isn't Count Dracula, but the doppelganger-superior! And he's raising his crossbow!

"Speaking of foul tricks," the doppelganger-superior says, aiming his crossbow at Hexum. "I should have known. You're using mind tricks to make us believe there's a mummy. But it's not real."

"Hexum, look out!" I yell.

THWIP!

"Arrrgh!" Hexum yells as the arrow strikes him square in the back.

"Crawler!" I yell. "Hexum was shot! We have to go back!"

"N-No!" Hexum barks, his voice cracking. "Go! Get him out of here! N-Now!"

"I'm sorry, kid," Crawler says. "Orders are orders."

"No!" I cry as Crawler pulls me up into the tunnel.

The last thing I see are Hexum's eyes.

Ten

His sad, green eyes.

"Fools!" Count Dracula yells. "Get the boy!"

AWWWOOOO!

Werewolves!

The werewolves are coming!

Seconds later, the first one enters the tunnel, followed by three more! We can't outrun them! But then—

YELP!

The werewolves scream and jump back frightened as a ball of fire erupts in front of the pack! But I know the truth. Hexum is helping us escape!

Crawler picks up his pace and the diversion gives us enough time to cover some serious distance. And then, just as quickly as the fire came, I hear Hexum SCREAM, and the flame flickers out.

And that's when I know.

He's dead.

Hexum is… dead.

He sacrificed himself… so I could live.

I choke back tears and flinch as sunlight hits my eyes. We're outside the cave now and Crawler keeps on moving, crossing the rocky plains in no time flat. Then, he puts me in the jeep.

"Buckle up," he says, getting into the driver's seat.

And then he pounds the gas and we're off.

MONSTEROLOGY 101 FIELD GUIDE

DOPPELGANGER

CLASSIFICATION:

Type: Shapeshifter
Sub-Type: Superior
Height: Variable
Weight: Variable
Eye Color: Variable
Hair Color: Variable

KNOWN ABILITIES:

- A rare subtype of doppelganger
- With one touch, can replicate the surface characteristics of a victim, including their thoughts and innermost desires

KNOWN WEAKNESSES:

- Cannot mimic the special abilities of a victim
- Can only change into human forms, unable to take the form of animals or objects

DANGER LEVEL:
EXTREME

TIPS TO AVOID AN UNWANTED ENCOUNTER:

- It is nearly impossible to identify a Doppelganger-Superior
- If an individual is exhibiting slightly uncharacteristic behavior, they may have been replaced by a Doppelganger-Superior

CHAPTER ELEVEN

RAISING THE STAKES

As we pull into the academy, all I feel is numb.

Professor Hexum is dead.

Because of me.

His final scream keeps replaying in my head, haunting me. I'm still having a hard time processing it all. I mean, despite everything we've been through, in the end, he sacrificed his life to save mine.

Honestly, I don't think I've ever been such a terrible judge of character. Hexum said I didn't have to like him, but his job was to make me stronger so I could defeat Count Dracula. He told me that's why he's harder on me than the other kids. He was always on my side, but I just couldn't see it.

And now I hate myself for it.

Crawler had little to say on the ride home, but as he pulls around the circular driveway, he finally says—

"Listen, Bram. I know things are difficult right now, but we need to get everyone together to tell them what happened. Why don't you head up to the auditorium and

I'll meet you there? Can you do that?"

"Yeah," I say, staring absently out the windshield.

"Great," Crawler says. "I'll round everyone up and bring them to the auditorium. But don't worry, I'll do all of the talking, okay?"

"Yeah," I hear myself say. "Okay."

"See you soon," he says, and then he gets out of the jeep and slams the door behind him.

As I step out of the car it feels like I'm having an out of body experience. It's morning and the sun is shining but I don't care if I get burned. I don't care about anything right now. Strangely, I barely feel my feet walking across campus. Instead, it's like I'm floating across the quad.

As I climb up the front stairs and enter the building, I see the school banner hanging up high. It reads:

YOU MUST BELIEVE IN THINGS YOU CANNOT IMAGINE

Isn't that the truth.

It's crazy how much has happened that I couldn't imagine. Like, the last time I walked through this entranceway I was with Van Helsing. Or at least I thought it was Van Helsing. Now I'm kicking myself for not realizing he was a doppelganger. I should have been more aware. I should have figured it out.

But I didn't.

Eleven

And now the real Van Helsing is in Count Dracula's evil hands. Just thinking about what he must be going through makes me shudder. And I feel like such a fool for even considering the things Count Dracula said to me.

Why did I let him mess with my head? Count Dracula said Van Helsing was using me. That Van Helsing would destroy me once he was finished with me. But I don't believe him anymore.

After all, Van Helsing took me in when no one else would. Sure, we've had some trust issues, but every relationship has bumps in the road. Van Helsing was just trying to protect me, and now I know what I've got to do.

I've got to rescue Van Helsing.

I've got to destroy Count Dracula once and for all.

I open the doors to the empty auditorium and my mind flashes back to the last time I was here. It was when Van Helsing introduced Dr. Renfield as our new professor of Monster Mindset. I can still see him staring at me from the stage.

Then, as I step inside the auditorium, a realization hits me like a ton of bricks.

Dr. Renfield!

He's probably still here! Inside that crazy clock!

I've got to talk to him!

But as soon as I exit the auditorium, a wave of students are coming my way. Crawler must have sent them to hear the news about Van Helsing and Hexum. I'd love to stay here and support Crawler, but I need answers.

I push my way through the crowd when I hear—

"Bram?"

Then, I see Aura and Rage. Rage smiles when he sees me and I'm relieved he's back on his feet again, but I can't afford to stop and chit-chat.

"Hey," I say. "I'd love to join you guys, but I can't talk right now. I've got somewhere I've gotta be."

"Why do you look so stressed out?" Aura asks, looking at me funny. "And do you know why Crawler called this assembly?"

"Yeah," I say, "and it's horrible news. Look, when you said Van Helsing was off his rocker you weren't kidding."

"What does that mean?" she says.

Just then, Blobby bumps into me on his way to the auditorium and the rest of the Howler's laugh.

"Look," I say, ignoring them as I head for the stairs. "Just go inside. Crawler will tell you everything. If he asks where I am just tell him I had to go to the bathroom."

But instead of going to the auditorium, Aura and Rage follow me to the stairs.

"Okay," Aura says, floating beside me. "Clearly, you know what's going on, so save us Crawler's sugarcoated explanation and tell us what's really happening."

As we head downstairs I debate if I should give them the whole story. But as I look at their determined faces I realize the two of them have been by my side the entire

Eleven

time. I couldn't ask for better friends. So, I might as well give them the unfiltered truth.

"Here's the scoop," I say, stopping on the landing. "And it's really bad, so get ready."

"Okay," they say in unison.

"Alright," I say, taking a deep breath. "Here it is. Last night, after you left, Van Helsing took Crawler, Hexum, and I to a cavern to recover a Supernatural object called the Crown of Souls before Count Dracula could get it. But it was a trap because Van Helsing wasn't Van Helsing at all, but rather a creature called a doppelganger-superior who led us right into the hands of Count Dracula and his minions. Count Dracula got the Crown of Souls first and would have killed me if it weren't for Hexum who created an illusion of a mummy that allowed Crawler and I to escape. But Hexum got shot by the doppelganger-superior and now… now he's dead."

Tears flood down my cheeks as I finish.

"What?" Rage says. "A-Are you serious?"

"Oh no," Aura says. "I'm so sorry, Bram."

"I can't believe it," Rage says, still stunned. "Are you sure Hexum is dead?"

"Yeah," I say. "And it's all my fault. Again."

"Bram, you can't take the blame for this," Aura says. "There's no way you could have known. I mean, that explains why Van Helsing was acting so out of character, but a doppelganger-superior? We studied those in

Holmwood's class. It replicates a person's physical characteristics and what they think and feel. It could fool anyone, and I guess that includes the Artifacts of Virtue."

"Yeah," I say. "That's clear now."

"What's the Crown of Souls?" Rage asks.

"It's an artifact that can resurrect you if you die," I say. "Your body and spirit."

"And Count Dracula has the Crown of Souls?" Aura says. "That's, like, bad news."

"You're telling me," I say.

"So, where are you going now?" Rage asks.

"To see Dr. Renfield," I answer.

"Renfield?" they say, looking at one another.

"Yeah," I say. "I know it sounds crazy but he's here, at the school. He's the one who told us about the Crown of Souls. He and that fake Van Helsing set me up, and now I want answers."

"Okay, then," Aura says. "Lead the way."

We finish going downstairs and then scoot across the entranceway into the faculty lounge wing. I lead them down the hall, past the kitchen, and stop in front of the grandfather clock. That's when I realize we may have a problem. When the fake Van Helsing took me here, the clock only opened up when it struck—

"Um, what are you doing?" Rage asks.

"Moving the minute hand to one minute before midnight," I say, standing on my tippy toes.

"Why?" he asks. "It's the middle of the morning."

[115]

Eleven

"You'll see," I say, stepping back.

We stare at the second-hand ticking around the face of the clock, until… DONG!

Suddenly, the front doors of the clock spring open.

"Whoa!" Rage says. "That's wild."

"You ain't seen nothing yet," I say, stepping inside.

Rage and Aura look awestruck as they follow me down the clock hallway until we reach the prison cell at the end. But their amazement quickly turns to shock when they spot the blindfolded Renfield inside.

"You weren't kidding," Rage whispers.

"Dr. Renfield," I say. "Are you surprised to hear my voice?"

"Bram?" he says, standing up and looking around. "Is that you? And was that Mr. Rage I heard as well?"

"Hi," Rage says.

"It is nice to hear your voice," Dr. Renfield says, feeling his way over to the barred door. "Should I assume Ms. Aura is here as well?"

"Check," Aura says.

"The three musketeers," Dr. Renfield says. "It is such a pleasure to be with you all again."

"Knock it off," I say. "You know you set us up. Count Dracula nearly killed me and Professor Hexum is dead because of you."

"Dead?" Dr. Renfield says, his eyebrows raised. "That was never my intention when I provided you with that information. I certainly hope you are okay and I am so sorry for your loss. I never liked Alastair Hexum, but I certainly never wished him dead. He was such a passionate teacher."

"What's with him?" Rage whispers.

He is acting weird, but then I remember why.

"Last night Professor Morris gave him a truth serum," I whisper. "Maybe it's still in his system."

"Well," Aura whispers. "test him."

Right. I try to think of something to ask him, and then I remember our conversation in the gymnasium when he was still a teacher here.

"Dr. Renfield," I say, "when you asked me if I knew where the Spear of Darkness was, were you working for Count Dracula?"

"Yes, I was," Dr. Renfield says without hesitation. "I was completely under his influence."

Aura and Rage look at each other.

"I thought so," I say. "But it's good to hear you admit it. Here's another one. Were you aware that Van Helsing was a doppelganger-superior?"

"A doppelganger-superior?" Dr. Renfield says, looking genuinely surprised. "No, I was not aware of that nor did I suspect it was even a possibility."

"Interesting," I say. "So, you're saying you had no idea Van Helsing was a fake when you told us about the Crown of Souls?"

"No," Dr. Renfield says. "None at all."

Well, that's interesting. I guess he was as clueless

Eleven

about the trap as we were.

"I've got one," Aura says. "Do you know where Count Dracula is hiding out? Where his base of operations is located?"

"No, I'm afraid not," Dr. Renfield says. "Count Dracula always visited me, usually in the middle of the night. I never visited him."

"Drat," Aura says.

"Well," Rage says. "This is useless. Let's go."

But as I think back to the conversation Dr. Renfield and I had about the Spear of Darkness, I also remember him saying that Van Helsing had other Supernatural objects here at the academy. And that gives me an idea.

"Hang on," I say. "Did Van Helsing ever tell you if he had any other Supernatural artifacts in his possession that could help us defeat Count Dracula?"

"Why yes," Dr. Renfield says. "He did."

The three of us look at one another.

"Really?" I say. "Like what?"

"Well, I recall him telling me once about another artifact," Dr. Renfield says. "He called it… the Eternal Stake. He said it was whittled from the Tree of Life itself, and if it struck a vampire it could destroy their mortal body with just one blow."

The Eternal Stake?

For a second, I'm flabbergasted. I mean, Van Helsing never mentioned anything about an Eternal Stake. Then, I get a frightening thought. Did he keep it from me because he was planning to use it on me?

"Interesting," Aura says. "I've never heard of it. Did he tell you where he kept this 'Eternal Stake?'"

"No," Dr. Renfield says. "Except he did say he was keeping it warm, just in case he needed to use it."

Keeping it warm? What's that supposed to mean?

"Is there, um, anything else you think we should know?" I ask. "You know, like any other secret vampire-destroying weapons Van Helsing was hiding?"

"No," Dr. Renfield says. "That was all. But now that I have helped you, maybe you can help me? Can you let me out of this cage?"

"Um, no," I say. "Sorry."

"I understand," he says sadly, slinking down to the ground. "I wouldn't let myself out either. But perhaps you would be willing to do me a favor. I'm quite hungry. Would you be able to get me a sandwich?"

"Sure," I say. "No problem. Thanks for your help."

"It was my pleasure," Dr. Renfield says. "Good luck. It was great speaking with all of you."

As we make our way back down the clock hallway, no one says a word. Then, we reenter the main building.

"Well, that was unexpected," Aura says finally.

"Yeah," I say. "You're telling me. But strangely, despite everything Dr. Renfield's done, I believe him."

"What's the Tree of Life anyway?" Rage asks.

"The Tree of Life is a mythical tree known throughout ancient cultures," Aura says. "Different

Eleven

civilizations might call it different things, but they all see it as the source of spiritual and physical life."

"Right," Rage says. "So, what do we do now?"

"Duh," Aura says. "We find the Eternal Stake. I bet it's here somewhere, just like the Spear of Darkness was. Something tells me Van Helsing would want to keep something that powerful close at hand. What do you think, Bram?"

I hear Aura talking, but I'm lost in thought. I just can't shake the feeling Van Helsing didn't tell me about the Eternal Stake for a reason. But what was the reason?

"Bram?" Aura says. "Don't you think we should find the Eternal Stake?"

"Um, yeah," I say. "Totally. We need to get right on that. But first I've got to take care of this."

I push through the doors of the faculty kitchen.

"Where are you going?" Rage asks.

"To find a cafeteria imp," I say. "I promised Dr. Renfield a sandwich."

CHAPTER TWELVE

RELATIVELY SPEAKING

The Eternal Stake.

I still don't understand why Van Helsing never told me about it. I mean, having a weapon that can destroy the mortal body of a vampire with one blow seems like something he'd want to share. Unless, of course, he was planning to use it on me.

I inhale deeply and breathe out.

I don't know what to think anymore.

Whatever Van Helsing's intentions were, Rage, Aura, and I turned the academy upside down searching for the Eternal Stake. But there was so much ground to cover we had to split up. Rage searched Monster House, Aura covered the faculty residences, and I scoured the main building.

But no one found it.

Now Rage and I are back in our room exhausted while Aura is still out there looking. I wish I had the stamina of a ghost, but my feet are throbbing and it wouldn't surprise me if they fell off.

Twelve

I was so confident I was going to find the Eternal Stake in Van Helsing's office but it didn't happen. Not that I'm surprised. There's so much clutter in there it's hard to move around, let alone find an Eternal Stake in a proverbial haystack. Between the mountains of books, half-finished inventions, and medieval weaponry it was probably a lost cause from the start.

Speaking of lost causes, I was pretty much an emotional wreck as soon as I entered Van Helsing's office. But I really lost it when I saw his empty chair by the fireplace. I remembered all the times I sat across from him, soaking in his wisdom as he fed logs into the fire.

But now his fire is out.

So, I didn't find the Eternal Stake. It probably didn't help that I have no idea what it looks like. I mean, a stake is a stake, right?

Unless, of course, it's not.

As I've come to learn when you're dealing with the Supernatural, nothing is as it seems. I mean, who would have thought that Van Helsing wasn't actually Van Helsing but a doppelganger-superior? Or that Hexum's walking stick was really the Spear of Darkness?

Every time I think of Hexum I feel incredible guilt. He sacrificed himself to save me, and what am I doing to honor his sacrifice? Sitting on my bed like a useless lump.

Some hero I turned out to be.

I look at Rage's innocent face. I don't think I could live with myself if something happened to him or Aura or my other friends. This all started because of me and I'm the one who's going to have to finish it.

Alone.

"Um, Bram," Rage says, sitting up in his bed.

"Yeah," I say. "What is it?"

"Well," he says, "remember when I told you I checked Monster House from top to bottom?"

"Yeah," I say.

"Well, I didn't check the 'real' bottom," Rage says.

The 'real' bottom? For a second I'm confused, but then it dawns on me what he's talking about.

"You mean, the forbidden basement?" I say.

"Yeah, that bottom," he says.

Just thinking about the forbidden basement sends a chill down my spine. I went down there to prove that the Artifacts of Virtue existed, and I barely made it out alive. Could Van Helsing have hidden the Eternal Stake in the basement?

I guess it's possible, but I do remember it being pretty cold down there. Didn't Dr. Renfield say Van Helsing liked to keep the Eternal Stake warm, in case he needed to—

Warm?

Holy cow!

I know where it is! I can't believe I missed it!

"Don't be mad at me," Rage continues. "I-I didn't really forget to look down there, but I didn't want to go down there alone. And I don't want to go down n—"

Twelve

"Don't worry about it," I say, hopping off my bed. "The Eternal Stake isn't down there. But I think I know where it is."

"You do?" Rage says. "Where?"

"I've got to go," I say, grabbing my hoodie. "You stay here."

"Stay here?" Rage says, jumping off his bed. "Forget it. I'm coming with you. And shouldn't we get Aura?"

But I don't answer him. Instead, I turn on my super-speed and bolt down the stairs, leaving him in the dust. I feel bad not bringing him along, but I've hurt enough people. Going forward, I need to handle this on my own.

Within seconds, I'm outside the main building.

And that's when I run into Crawler.

"Bram?" he says, exiting through the double doors.

Uh-oh. I'm sure he's upset with me for missing his assembly but I can't let him know what I'm up to.

"Where are you off to at top speed?" he says. "I'm sure you heard that I suspended all classes for the time being. The main building is closed."

"Closed?" I say. Well, I guess I missed out on that little tidbit when I skipped the assembly. But I have to get inside. "Right, but I um, think I left my backpack in the gymnasium when we had exams. So, I thought I'd check and see if it's there. I'll be quick."

"No problem," Crawler says. "But I'm glad we ran into each other. I intended to speak with you after the assembly but couldn't find you."

"Yeah," I say. "Sorry about that."

"Hey, it's okay," Crawler says. "I just want to make sure you're okay. That battle in the cavern was... intense, and you've been through a lot."

"Yeah," I say. "You could say that."

"I know," he says, patting me on the shoulder with one of his spider legs. "But, well, now that Van Helsing isn't here, we need to talk about the future."

"The future?" I say.

"Yes," he says. "The professors and I were talking, and you're going to need more guidance now than ever before. No one here expects you to pick up the pieces and figure out what to do on your own. We're fighting a war, and we need to fight it together. So, the professors and I are going to band together to counsel you."

"Oh," I say, with obvious surprise in my voice.

I mean, I appreciate what he's trying to do, but I've already decided that enough is enough. Once I find the Eternal Stake, it'll be time to do what I do best, which is go solo. So, it's time to get out of this conversation.

"That sounds great," I say.

"I'm glad to hear you say that," Crawler says with a smile. "We'll get through this, Bram. Now go see if your backpack is there, and then I'll meet you over at Monster House in about a half-hour. Deal?"

"Deal," I say, faking a smile.

As Crawler walks away I breathe a sigh of relief. For a second there I thought he was going to stop me for good.

Twelve

As soon as I enter the building I take off again. I have to say it does feel weird that no one is around. At this late hour, you'd usually see kids coming and going from their extracurricular activities. But now the place is empty.

That is, until I hit the faculty wing.

"P-Professor Seward!" I say, screeching to a halt.

The portly professor is standing in the hallway locking his door. And under his arm is a stack of exam booklets.

"Mr. Murray," he says, clearly surprised to see me. "What are you doing here? The main building is closed."

Not again.

"Yes," I say, scrambling for a good answer. I mean, it's not like I can tell him the same story I just told Crawler. I'm nowhere near the gym. "I know. I'm, um, just making sure there are no students left in the building. Trying to help out in any way I can."

"I see," Professor Seward says. "Well, I am looking forward to reading your exam essay this evening."

"My exam essay?" I say, surprised.

"Why yes, Mr. Murray, your exam essay," he says, holding up the exam booklets. "We may be in a war, but we must ensure we are delivering upon our high academic standards."

"Right," I say, kind of shocked he's even bringing this up right now. "Of course. Well, I, um, hope you enjoy it. Mine might be a little brief, but it's very profound."

"Excellent," he says. "Well then, I have a busy night ahead of me. Good evening Mr. Murray."

"Yes, good evening," I say.

As I watch Seward disappear around the corner I realize he'd be one of my counselors, and that just solidifies why I can't stick around. I wait until his footsteps fade away and then get down to business.

I approach Van Helsing's office and put my hand on the door. It's usually warm to the touch but not tonight. I peer over my shoulder to make sure I'm alone and then mist through the crevices of the doorframe.

Once inside I float over Van Helsing's mess until I reach the large room in the back. I collect my molecules near the fireplace and transform back to kid-form. I can't believe I missed it the first time, but now I've put all the clues together.

Renfield said Van Helsing kept the Eternal Stake 'warm' in case he needed to use it. Well, there's nowhere on campus warmer than his fireplace, and since he would only use the Eternal Stake on a vampire it all fits together. Van Helsing must have kept the Eternal Stake close at hand for our fireside chats just in case he needed to use it—on me!

Just thinking about it makes me sick.

And if I'm right, I guess it answers the question once and for all if Van Helsing ever trusted me. Not that I could blame him if he didn't. I mean, maybe he was just trying to protect himself. After all, I could become a bloodsucking vampire at any moment.

Now I just need to find it.

Twelve

I get on my hands and knees and look under his chair but don't see anything. Then, I stick my head in the unlit fireplace and look around but still nothing. Come on, where would I find a wooden—

Wooden?

Man, am I a dufus or what?

What's wooden and near a fireplace?

Logs!

I inspect the log holder next to the fireplace. There are a bunch of jagged, axe-cut logs stacked inside an iron holder, but they all look the same. Then, I notice one log on the very bottom that looks quite different. Unlike the others, this one has a round, smooth bottom.

I pull it and it slides out easily, like it wasn't part of the pile at all but sitting inside a separate holder. And as I turn it in my hands, it's smooth, brown, and has a sharp point on one end.

It's a stake!

But it looks kind of ordinary.

Is it a stake, or is it the Eternal Stake?

Then, I notice Van Helsing's chair is right next to the log holder. All he would need to do is reach back with his right arm and grab it. I never would have seen it coming.

Well, this has to be it, so it's time to get moving. But as I start to head out something catches my eye. There's a folder lying on the floor next to Van Helsing's desk. I must have knocked it off when I was going through his stuff earlier.

I reach down to pick it up when I see the corner of a yellowed paper sticking out. Curious, I open the folder and see an old student assessment profile from years earlier. And attached to it is a black and white photograph of a boy who is a little older than me. He has dark hair, dark eyes, pointy ears, and... fangs?

And then I read his name and my heart stops.

GABRIEL MURRAY

G-Gabriel Murray? But that's... my dad?

I blink hard and look at the photo again. I mean, I've never actually seen a picture of my dad before. I put the profile on the desk and trace his features with my index finger. I-I can't believe how much I look like him.

Then, I read through his profile. We're about the same height and weight, and according to these scores, no one other than Van Helsing thought he was a good candidate for the academy.

I wonder why Van Helsing never showed this to me. And why was he looking at my father's profile in the first place? He must have pulled it out before he went to New York City.

"Bram?"

"Ahh!" I scream!

My heart is pounding, and when I look up I see Aura floating there. I close the folder.

"How did you get in here?" I ask.

Twelve

"Seriously?" she says. "I'm a ghost, remember? Rage told me you took off like a lunatic to find the Eternal Stake. So, I figured you probably came here." Then, she sees the stake in my hand. "Is that it?"

"I think so," I say, holding it up. "It was in the log holder next to the fireplace."

"Keeping it 'warm,'" Aura says. "Just like Renfield said. That's great news. And I have some good news myself."

"Really?" I say, "what's that?"

"Well," she says. "I tapped into the spirit network and we finally figured out where that first shipment from Romania went. Sleepy Hollow, New York."

"Sleepy Hollow?" I say. "As in, the Legend of Sleepy Hollow? As in, the creepy story with the Headless Horseman? That's a real place?"

"Yep," she says. "As real as you and I. The cargo was delivered from the port to an abandoned estate in Sleepy Hollow, and I'm guessing that's where we'll find Count Dracula."

"Great job," I say. "Just give me the address and I'll get going."

"You'll get going?" Aura says, crossing her arms. "Bram, what are you talking about? The rest of the team are outside and we're going with you. We have to save Van Helsing."

"No," I say. "It's too dangerous. I... I won't let anyone else I care about get hurt. I'm going alone."

[130]

"Don't be stupid, Bram," she says. "This is Count Dracula and the Dark Ones we're talking about. You're going to need help. Look, I know you're upset about Hexum and Van Helsing. We all are. But it doesn't mean you should run off and do something stupid. Look, we may not be ready, but we're a team and we stick together. Besides, I'm the one who knows where we're going, remember?"

Well, she's got me there.

We stare at each other in silence. Unfortunately, she's probably right. Taking on Count Dracula and the Dark Ones alone would be suicide. And it would be nice to have their company. But I can't let anyone else get hurt. So, once we get where we need to go, I'll do my thing.

"Fine," I say. "But only because you're holding the location hostage."

"Perfect," she says. "Now get ready, because Hairball is driving again."

"Wonderful," I say. "I'll grab my barf bag."

And as she turns to leave, I take my dad's profile out of the folder, fold it in half, and slip it into my hoodie pocket.

CHAPTER THIRTEEN

ALMOST THERE

"We're here," Aura says. "Slow down, Hairball."

Thank goodness because I'm not feeling so hot.

At first, I thought it was Hairball's typically terrible driving, but now I'm not so sure. Unlike the other roller coaster rides he's taken us on, the problem this time isn't my stomach but my head, which is pounding. I'd love to just lay down and chill but there's no room in the back of this cramped jeep. Besides, there's no time for rest.

It's showtime.

I turn the Eternal Stake in my hands. I sure hope it's ready because I know I'm not. After all, everybody here thinks our mission is to rescue Van Helsing. I'd like that too, but I also have another more personal mission.

I'm going to destroy Count Dracula.

"Um, is that the place?" Rage asks, pressing into my arm as he leans forward to look out the front windshield. "Because it's, like, super creepy."

"Yep, that's the place," Aura says, checking her map. "Right in the heart of Sleepy Hollow. Hairball, stop

Thirteen

driving, and pull over already. I said we're here."

"Okay, okay," Hairball says. "No need to get sassy."

As Hairball steers us to the side of the road and parks, I look out the passenger-side window. We're high on an empty mountain road overlooking a massive estate. But as I take it all in, I think Rage undersold the place because it's way more than super creepy, it's downright frightening.

The estate has acres of greenery surrounding a stately old manor, which would have been lovely if the greenery weren't swampland and the manor wasn't falling down. In fact, with the black vines clawing the exterior, plywood covering the windows, and grotesque statues weighing down the roof, I'm not sure how the manor is still standing. The whole vibe feels dark and empty, just like the evil vampire living inside.

"My, what a charming home," InvisiBill says. "Now how about we keep driving until we find a pizza place?"

"That's enough, you cowards," Aura says. "Everybody out of the jeep. Our headmaster is in trouble and we're going to get him out of there. Now stop complaining."

"But I love complaining," InvisiBill says.

"Shut it." Aura responds.

"Message received," InvisiBill says.

As we step out of the jeep, Kat sniffs the air and says, "That's weird, it smells like gas."

"Sorry," Stanphibian says.

"What?" Kat says. "No, not that kind of gas, but yuck. No, it smells like—"

CLICK!

Suddenly, we're blinded by a massive spotlight!

I turn away, shielding my eyes, but the light is so intense it's making my headache worse!

"Hello, monsters," comes a familiar female voice. "Long time no see."

"Agent M?" I say, and when I squint I see a tall, thin silhouette coming towards us. "What are you doing here?"

"Funny, I was going to ask you the same thing," she says, stopping several feet away. "We've been tracking your vehicle since you left the Van Helsing Academy, and let me tell you, your driving is horrific. But let's get to the point. You monsters did a heck of a job damaging our headquarters. My boss is even threatening to cut my budget to make the repairs. So guess what? It's payback time. But before things get ugly for you, I'm curious why you pulled over in the middle of nowhere."

"Turn off the light and I'll tell you," I say.

There are a few seconds of silence, and then—

"Cut the spotlight!" Agent M commands.

The spotlight CLICKS off and it takes a few seconds to stop seeing stars, but that's not my biggest problem right now. I wasn't expecting Agent M and her agents to show up and I can't let her stop me from getting inside that manor. I mean, they could take us down quickly.

Thirteen

This is so annoying.

I'm so close to Count Dracula, but I might never get to him because of DSI. But then again, maybe that's the answer. If she thinks I'm as bad as Count Dracula then I'll give her exactly what she wants. I'll show her what a real vampire can do.

Wait, what?

That wasn't me thinking those thoughts, was it?

"You have one minute," Agent M says, looking at her watch. "One minute to explain yourselves before I unleash a world of hurt."

"Bram?" Aura says. "Are you okay?"

"Yeah," I say, rubbing my forehead. Where did those thoughts even come from?

"Forty seconds," Agent M says, tapping her watch.

"Look," I say. "I-I know we didn't get off on the right foot the first time, but please hear me out because it was all a big misunderstanding. We want to stop Count Dracula as badly as you do. And based on our detective work we've determined he's inside that manor over there, and he's holding our headmaster prisoner."

"Count Dracula?" Agent M says, looking over at the estate. "You're saying he's in that abandoned building?"

"Yep," Aura says. "The first cargo shipment from Romania was delivered to that address."

"Really?" Agent M says skeptically. "And how did you figure that out? We have the best agents in the world and they couldn't trace the cargo."

"I'm guessing your agents aren't ghosts," Aura says, flipping her hair.

"I see," Agent M says, looking down at her watch. "Well, time's up. Hit the spotlight, boys!"

CLICK!

The spotlight flashes again, and as I turn away from the light I see something moving on the roof of the manor. In fact, lots of large, gray things are moving on the rooftop. And that's when it hits me.

Those grotesque statues!

They were never statues at all!

They're... gargoyles!

Just then, one unfurls its stony wings and looks our way. Holy cow! It's the spotlight! It's like a homing signal!

"Turn off the light!" I yell, pointing towards the manor. "It's attracting the gargoyles!"

"Gargoyles?" Agent M says with a laugh, looking at the manor. "Nice try, kid, but... Uh-oh."

"Monstrosities, move out!" I yell.

"DSI!" Agent M yells. "Get ready to rumble!"

Rage, Aura, and I cluster together and bolt down the side of the mountain as the rest of the team scampers the other way. We stumble down the rocky landscape until we hit the bottom and duck into the woods. Looking up, I see a gigantic shape fly above the trees, and then—

KABOOM! KABOOM!

Massive explosions erupt overhead as artillery shrapnel rains down from the sky.

Thirteen

"We've got to get to the manor!" I yell.

We slog our way through the murky swamp, but it's so deep I'm soaked up to my thighs. I cover my ears as more explosions go off overhead.

"What's happening?" Rage says, struggling to move through the swamp which is up to his waist.

"DSI is fighting the gargoyles," Aura says, floating above the swamp surface. "I hope the others got away."

I do too, but it's not like we can stop and check.

Count Dracula definitely knows we're coming now.

I grip the Eternal Stake tight. I can't afford to lose this baby. And then I remember what's inside my pocket. I reach into my hoodie and feel the folded paper inside. Whew, it's still there. I don't know why, but it feels good to have my dad with me, even if it's just his old school profile.

"Bram!" Aura yells, pointing up. "Look out!"

Just then, I hear SNAPPING from overhead as thick branches come crashing to the ground, followed by a massive figure splashing down in front of us! Suddenly, I'm drenched in dirty swamp water.

I wipe my eyes with my sleeve and when my vision clears, I'm staring at a ten-foot-tall, winged gargoyle. He fixes me with his bulging eyes and flexes his gigantic stone muscles!

"Scatter!" I yell.

The gargoyle leaps at me and I dive out of the way as he plows into a massive tree behind me, knocking it over like it was a bowling pin. But as I pull myself out of the swamp, he gets back up.

"We've got to stop him!" Aura yells. "All this noise will bring more gargoyles!"

She's right about that. But the question is how? And then I realize I don't see Rage. Where'd he go?

POW!

There's an explosion of rock, and the gargoyle goes flying back into another tree! And when I look over to see who punched him, I find myself staring at another ten-foot monster, but this one has blonde hair and purple skin!

It's Rage!

"RRRAAAGGGEEE FFFIIIGGGHHHTTT!"

I-I can't believe it! Rage turned himself into Monster Rage to protect us!

The gargoyle rolls over and there's a massive hole in his chest. Honestly, with a wound like that, I can't believe he's still moving. But then he arches his back and SCREECHES into the night air.

"Stop him!" Aura yells. "He's calling for help!"

Rage marches over, raises his big foot, and STOMPS.

The screeching ends.

But it's too late.

We hear more branches SNAPPING from above, and two more gargoyles drop from the sky!

This is not good.

"GO!" Rage barks at us. "RRAAGGEE

Thirteen

FFIIGGHHTT!"

"Are you crazy?" I say. "We can't leave you!"

"Bram, let's go!" Aura yells, waving me on. "He's got this! We've got to save Van Helsing."

I hesitate for a second, but as Rage socks another gargoyle I realize Aura is right. I'm so proud of him. He's got this whole situation under control. He's finally mastered the beast inside.

The question is, can I do the same thing?

As we get closer to the manor we find ourselves engulfed in a thick fog. I stick close to Aura so I don't lose her, but when I look at the manor in the distance, I see something else coming through the fog—a furry, hunched figure with long arms and pointy ears. And then I spot another. And another. And another.

Werewolves!

I scan the horizon and see a whole army of them!

"Aura!" I yell. "Werewolves coming fast!"

"Got it," Aura says, stopping. "This one is mine."

"What?" I say. "There's like, twenty of them."

"And none of them can touch me," she says. "Look, let's make this simple. You go to mist-form and blend into the fog while I create a distraction to pull them away from you. Then, you go rescue Van Helsing. Got it?"

"You're kidding right?" I say. But when I look at the manor the werewolves have gotten much closer. I turn back to object to Aura's grand plan but she's gone!

"OVER HERE, SUCKERS!" comes Aura's voice

from far away. "CATCH ME IF YOU CAN!"

ARRRROOOOO!

That was a howl! I go to mist-form and see the werewolves gathering only twenty feet away. One of them SNARLS and the pack takes off in hot pursuit. Once they're gone I go back to kid-form. I've got to hand it to Aura, she might be the bravest monster I know.

I start for the manor when something tackles me from the side! We tumble into the swamp and I kick up my leg, using our momentum to flip my attacker over my body. Then, I get to my feet, spitting swamp water out of my mouth. And that's when I realize my hands are empty.

The Eternal Stake! It's gone!

That's bad, but I've got an even bigger problem right now because I'm staring at a soaking wet werewolf. Clearly, Aura didn't fool this one and I curse myself for not staying in mist-form. But I don't have time for fun and games right now.

Suddenly, I spot a sharp, wooden object floating in the swamp between us. It's the Eternal Stake!

Unfortunately, the werewolf tracks my eyes and sees it too. It's gonna be a foot race. We both jump for it at the same time, but I turn on my super-speed and beat the werewolf to the spot. I grab the Eternal Stake and clear out as the werewolf dives headfirst into the swamp.

Okay, it's time to get back on track. I concentrate hard and go back to mist-form. The werewolf resurfaces and looks around for me, but I'm not planning on telling

Thirteen

him where I went. That was too close for comfort and the last mistake I can afford.

Fooling a werewolf is one thing but fooling Count Dracula won't be so easy. As I drift away towards the manor, I hear the werewolf HOWLING in frustration.

From this point forward, I can't let anything stop me from completing my mission. I can't let anything stop me from destroying Count Dracula.

MONSTEROLOGY 101 FIELD GUIDE

GARGOYLE

CLASSIFICATION:

Type: Abnormal
Sub-Type: Demon
Height: Variable
Weight: Variable
Eye Color: Gray
Hair Color: None

KNOWN ABILITIES:

- Transform from stone statues
- Stony hide makes them nearly indestructable
- Deceptively agile when flying in the air

KNOWN WEAKNESSES:

- Not intelligent
- Large size makes them easy to spot in the air
- Some only come alive at night

DANGER LEVEL:
HIGH

TIPS TO AVOID AN UNWANTED ENCOUNTER:

- Avoid buildings typically decorated with gargoyle-like statues
- If in a city environment, remain indoors as much as possible

CHAPTER FOURTEEN

DOUBLE CROSS

I stay in mist-form until I reach the manor.

I breeze past a few more werewolf sentries and then flow through the cracks of a boarded-up window. It's unnaturally dark inside but I can see everything clearly. Based on the ornate molding and antique furniture, I'd say the place must have been pretty swanky back in its day. Unfortunately, in its present condition, it should probably be condemned.

The wood floors are buckled, the staircase has fallen, and hundreds of rats are living in every conceivable nook and cranny. Other than the vermin, I'd guess no one's lived here for decades.

At least, until now.

As I drift through the various rooms, I think back to my first day at the Van Helsing Academy. There was so much I didn't know about monsters, and so much I didn't know about myself. And now I'm here, about to realize the destiny I didn't even know I had.

I hear Van Helsing's voice in my head, *'Only a*

vampire can kill another vampire.'

I see the faces of all the people counting on me.

Aura, Rage, Van Helsing, even Johnny.

I can't let them down.

I won't let them down.

Count Dracula is here and I need to find him.

I look for signs of life as I float through the once-grand ballrooms and spacious hallways but don't see anything. There's not even a dish in the kitchen sink. Hmmm? If I were a vampire where would I be hiding?

Oh yeah, I am a vampire.

Then, I approach a room with a plaque that reads, 'Butler's Pantry,' and flow inside. That's when I spot something interesting. There's a closed door in the corner. In all of the rooms I've explored, this is the first closed door I've found. I hover beside it and listen but don't hear any noises coming from the other side.

In my gut, I'm sure this door leads to a dark and creepy basement, and nothing good ever happens in a dark and creepy basement. Truthfully, I'm terrified, but I push past the fear. After all, I've got a job to do.

So, I move through the crevices and find a stairway going—yep—straight down. I knew it! I hesitate over the top stair for a few seconds to gather my courage and then drift down the steep stairway.

It's darker down here than upstairs, and when I reach the bottom I'm in a large, stone chamber staring at a long, narrow box made of wood that makes my jaw drop.

Fourteen

It's a coffin!

My misty heart starts racing.

I've seen enough horror movies to know that a coffin like that is for one person and one person only—Count Dracula! Now's my chance! But the lid is closed so I don't know if he's in there or not.

I-I can't believe it. This is the moment I've been waiting for—and the moment I've been dreading the most. If Count Dracula is inside, then I'll have a chance to finish this once and for all.

Unless, of course, he finishes me first.

I can't be a mist for what I need to do next, so I move to ground level and transform back into a kid. But as soon as I rematerialize, my nostrils are flooded with a foul stench that makes me gag.

Yuck! Where have I smelled that before?

I try ignoring it but it's just so strong. Then, I remember the Eternal Stake! Whew, even though I traveled a long way in mist-form it rematerialized with me. I sure hope it works as advertised because if not, I'm in serious trouble.

Well, there's no turning back now. I take a deep breath and tiptoe cautiously over to the coffin, sweat pouring down my forehead. With every step, I keep expecting the lid to spring open and Count Dracula to pop out and attack me.

But I can't stop now. Strangely, the closer I get, the dizzier I feel. I don't know if it's the stench or my headache but both seem to be getting worse. Suddenly, the room feels like it's spinning. It takes all of my willpower to finally reach the coffin, but when I do I place one hand on the lid and raise the Eternal Stake with the other.

Ready or not, here I am.

I brace myself and throw open the lid, hoping to find Count Dracula lying peacefully inside, but instead all I see is dirt! But not just any dirt, the coffin is filled with the same maggot-infested dirt we found on the ship! Aura was right, this is where the cargo was delivered. And now I know where that horrible smell is coming from.

But where is—

"Welcome, Bram," comes a deep voice that sends shivers down my spine.

I spin around to find Count Dracula hanging upside down from the ceiling like a bat! I back away from the coffin and raise the Eternal Stake, but for some reason, I'm seeing double right now. I wouldn't know which Count Dracula to strike even if I tried.

"I see you are experiencing some dizziness," Count Dracula says. "Do not be alarmed, it is an expected reaction when you are first exposed to our homeland."

"Homeland?" I say. "What are you talking about?"

"The dirt inside my coffin," Count Dracula says calmly, dropping to the ground feet-first, his cape flowing behind him. "It is native soil from our homeland of Wallachia. It is essential for rest. Connecting with its

Fourteen

energy greatly renews my strength. It can be overwhelming at first, but soon enough it will become a great source of comfort to you. Now, you have had quite a challenging day. Perhaps you would like to rest in it?"

Rest in it? I glance over at the coffin. Strangely, other than the maggots and stench, it does look kind of comfortable. Almost like a dirt mattress. I bet it's pretty soft too.

Wait! What am I talking about? I shake my head. I-I don't know what I'm thinking right now. I'm dizzy and I feel myself getting… angrier.

"No way!" I yell, raising the Eternal Stake higher over my head. "I'm good. And Wallachia is NOT my homeland! Never was. Never will be."

"A pity," Count Dracula says shaking his head. "I see you have the Eternal Stake in your possession. I assume you are expecting to use it against me."

"You've got that right," I say. "Your evil ends now."

"You must be confident in its abilities," he says.

"Yeah," I say. "I am, but if you want to test it out come on over."

"You are either very brave or very foolish," Count Dracula says. And then he reaches into his cape and pulls out the Crown of Souls! As he puts it on his head, he says, "There, I believe we are even now. You with your artifact of destruction and me with my artifact of resurrection. We can fight if you wish, but it will end poorly for you."

I swallow hard. He's probably right about that. Either he'll destroy me or I'll destroy him, only to watch him get resurrected. And then I'll have to do it all over again. I'd call this a lose-lose situation!

What am I going to do? I need to stall. I've got to throw him off his game.

"You know, everyone thinks you're this big, bad guy," I say, "but deep down you're a coward at heart, aren't you?"

"What are you driveling on about?" Count Dracula sneers.

"You're a coward and you know it," I say. "You just hide in the shadows, manipulating the weak to get what you want. Remember Faustius, or Moreau, or Renfield? They were weak-minded and easy to control. And what about your war against mankind? You didn't even go to New York City to start your own war. You don't stick your neck out for anything because you're afraid to die, aren't you?"

"You know nothing about me," he says.

"I know a lot," I say. "And that's why you wanted the Crown of Souls, isn't it? You're afraid to die. And your quest for power is nothing more than you trying to save your own pitiful existence."

"Enough," Count Dracula says. "You know neither me nor your own mind! Here you stand, a monster in your own right, betraying your kind! Do you think humans will let you walk the streets in freedom when this is over? If you do you are a fool! They are, and always will be, afraid of what they cannot control, including you. They will hunt you down and destroy you, just as they have done to monsters like us for centuries."

I-I don't want to listen to what he's saying, but deep down I know he's right. I mean, I learned all about monster persecution in Seward's Supernatural history class. And Agent M and DSI are legitimate monster hunters who want nothing more than to capture me! I hadn't thought about it, but even if I win the battle against Count Dracula, no Naturals are going to throw us a parade. They'll just take us down next.

"Monsters can only stand with monsters," Count Dracula continues. "And your beloved headmaster is no exception. He will just as readily destroy you as he would me. I already know you question his motives."

I open my mouth to argue but nothing comes out.

He's right. I do question Van Helsing's motives. I mean, he never told me about the Eternal Stake in case he needed to use it against me.

Speaking of Van Helsing...

"Where is he?" I ask. "Where are you keeping him?"

"Still such blind loyalty?" Count Dracula says. "Well, you need not worry. He is here. Would you like to see him now? He has been waiting anxiously to see you."

"Yes," I say. But his sarcastic tone raises my alarm bells. What does he mean that Van Helsing has been waiting anxiously to see me?

"Very well," Count Dracula says, clasping his hands together. "Van Helsing, enter!"

The next thing I know, one of the doors opens and Van Helsing comes walking into the chamber! The good news is that he looks like he's okay, but the bad news is that he's aiming his Crossbow of Purity right at me!

"Headmaster?" I say. "What are you doing?"

"He is doing what I command," Count Dracula says.

"What?" I say. "What are you talking about?"

"Show him," Count Dracula says to Van Helsing.

Then, Van Helsing removes one hand from his crossbow and unwinds his scarf. And that's when I see two puncture wounds on the side of his neck!

Holy cow! Dracula bit him!

"Van Helsing is fully under my control," Count Dracula says, tapping his fingertips together. "Now, this will be most entertaining. Which of you will kill the other first?"

CHAPTER FIFTEEN

THE LAST AT BAT

I never expected this.

My eyes drift to the two puncture wounds on Van Helsing's neck. There's no doubt about it, that's a vampire bite, just like the one I saw on Renfield's neck.

And that can only mean one thing.

Count Dracula is controlling Van Helsing!

Staring down the barrel of Van Helsing's Crossbow of Purity puts everything in perspective. This whole mission was doomed from the start. There's no way I can defeat Count Dracula, especially since he has the Crown of Souls. And now he's gonna get the last laugh by watching me die at the hands of my mentor.

Nice going, Bram.

But I promised myself I wouldn't give up, no matter how dire the circumstances. If I don't figure something out right now then it's game over for me and mankind. So, let's take this one step at a time. And first up is breaking Count Dracula's influence over Van Helsing.

"Headmaster," I say calmly. "Please, don't shoot. It's

Fifteen

me, Bram. You remember me, don't you? Well, in case you forgot, I'm one of your students. You run an amazing academy that teaches monster kids how to be good so we can fight evil threats like Count Dracula over there. You are a kind and good man. You need to focus right now. You need to remember who you are."

Just then, Van Helsing's bushy eyebrows quiver.

"Fool," Count Dracula says, his lips curling into a menacing smile. "Your words have no meaning. Van Helsing is under my control now. Hear me, Van Helsing. Your ancestors have dedicated their pathetic lives to exterminating vampires, and now you have one in your sights. Destroy the child, Van Helsing! Make your ancestors proud!"

Van Helsing furrows his brow and lines up his crossbow to shoot me right through the heart. I-I can't believe it. I've lost him… and everything else.

"Shoot!" Count Dracula barks. "Get rid of our pest!"

"Yes, master," Van Helsing says robotically. "I will."

I brace myself for impact as Van Helsing's trigger finger twitches, but suddenly he wheels on Count Dracula and fires!

The villain's eyes light up and he disappears in a cloud of black mist! The silver arrow passes through harmlessly, scattering wisps everywhere.

"Devil!" Van Helsing shouts into the air. "You never controlled me and you never will! Bram, raise the Eternal Stake. It is time to end this."

A wave of adrenaline rushes through me as I realize that somehow Van Helsing is back—and he's on my side! But as Van Helsing reloads, the King of Darkness rematerializes right behind him.

"Headmaster!" I call out.

But it's too late.

"Yes, we will end this," Count Dracula says, lifting a surprised Van Helsing over his head like he weighs nothing. "Starting with you!"

Then, Count Dracula slams Van Helsing onto the stone floor. Van Helsing lands with a sickening thud and his arms flail across his body like a rag doll, sending the Crossbow of Purity clattering across the room.

"No!" I cry, rushing to Van Helsing's side.

His eyes are closed and there's a trickle of blood flowing from the corner of his mouth, but thankfully he's still breathing—barely.

"Monster!" I yell.

"Yes, I am," Count Dracula says, dusting off his cape, "and so are you. As you can see, nothing will stand in my way, including you. But I am feeling generous, so I will give you one last chance. Will you continue to be subservient to Naturals or will you embrace your true destiny? The world's greatest vampire-hunter is at your feet. Finish him and show me you have chosen wisely."

"What?" I say, getting to my feet. "Are you nuts? The only person I'm gonna finish is you!"

"Very well," Count Dracula says with a smirk. "Your

Fifteen

choice is made and your life must end. Though I must admit, I am curious to see how men taught a monster to fight."

As we circle each other, my heart is pounding out of my chest. I can't believe this moment I've been thinking about non-stop for months is actually happening. All of my fears are being realized.

And only one of us will come out alive.

Whoever wins will destroy the other's body and spirit for all of eternity!

Except I'm at a serious disadvantage. Not only is Count Dracula wearing the Crown of Souls, but he's also stronger, faster, and several-hundred-years more experienced than I am. I swallow hard. This shouldn't even be close.

Yet, he hasn't attacked me.

And that's when I realize I have something he's afraid of—something that's keeping him at bay.

The Eternal Stake.

Then, I remember what Renfield told me. Even though he's got the Crown of Souls, he's afraid of dying again. I mean, it took centuries for him to come back the first time and I'm guessing you don't forget something like that too easily.

Then, it dawns on me.

Just like I don't know if this Eternal Stake will work, he probably doesn't trust what's sitting on his head either? So maybe I can use that to my advantage.

"Boy, I sure hope the Crown of Souls is real," I say, "because wouldn't it stink to die again, but this time forever?"

"I think you should be the one concerned with dying," he says.

"I'm good," I say. "Because I've got this!"

I lunge at him with the Eternal Stake, but when I strike he easily sidesteps me and I get a face full of cape.

Okay, this isn't going to be easy. But maybe he's right. If I'm going to defeat him, it won't be by using what men taught me. Maybe I need to use what he taught me.

It's time to go vampire-ninja!

I turn into a mist, kick on my super-speed, and race behind him, but as soon as I rematerialize he goes into mist-form and dissipates before I strike. When he reappears, I turn into a bat and divebomb him, but he goes into bat-form and glides to the other side of the room as I crash into the wall.

"I am impressed," he says, buffing his black nails. "Your skills have improved, but this could take all evening."

"I've got time," I say, turning back to kid-form.

But while he doesn't look like he's even broken a sweat, I'm totally exhausted. If I don't get a lucky strike sometime soon I'm going to run out of energy.

And then I'll be easy pickings.

"Unfortunately," Count Dracula says, "I do not have that kind of time to spare. You see, I have a world to conquer, and once it is mine I will have an endless supply of blood to sustain me. So, I am afraid we will need to bring this to a tidy conclusion immediately."

Um, immediately?

But before I can react he becomes a blur, and the next thing I know, he's by my side, wrestling for control of the Eternal Stake! His fingers are like iron rods, digging into my wrists to pry the weapon free from my grasp! I try knocking him back with my thigh but he's too strong!

His face is so close I can smell his hot, putrid breath. If I can just angle the point of the Eternal Stake towards him, I might be able to jam it into his stomach. But he's so strong he's turning it towards me! I'm barely managing to hold him off, but I don't know for how long!

"Release the stake!" Count Dracula commands.

"N-Never!" I say.

Then, he unhinges his jaw, opens his mouth wide, and bites me in the left shoulder!

"AAAGGGHHH!" I yell as intense pain shoots through my body.

I react instinctively, SLAMMING my head into his. I scream again as his fangs release from my skin and we both fall to the ground disoriented. I sit up as soon as I land and grab my burning shoulder, only to feel a warm, wet liquid streaming down my arm. Holy cow! He bit all the way through! I'm bleeding all over the place!

Suddenly, my entire body feels hot and achy, like a fever is taking over. Yet, despite all of that, I'm somehow still holding the Eternal Stake. And when I look over at Count Dracula he's back on his feet, adjusting the Crown of Souls and licking his lips.

"There," he says, his voice echoing inside my head. *"Now I will take complete control and this will finally be over."*

N-No! He's in my head. And then I realize, with that bite he's bonded to me even more!

"Be a good boy and hand me the Eternal Stake," he says, walking towards me. *"I will be merciful when I end your life. Or not."*

N-No!

Yet, despite my protest, my arm is rising like it isn't even part of my body. Holy cow! This is what happened in the forbidden basement when he made me open that vault door! But this feels ten times more intense. I-I can't stop it!

"Yes," he says, inside my head.

And before I know it, my arm is fully extended, my palm is opening, and I'm offering him the Eternal Stake like it's on a silver platter!

"Thank you," Count Dracula says, reaching for it. "I will make your end quick and painful."

But then something catches my eye.

There's... a gray mist, swirling behind Count Dracula. W-What is that?

And just as Count Dracula is about to wrap his hand around the Eternal Stake, the gray mist circles rapidly and

Fifteen

knocks the Crown of Souls clear off his head!

"What?" Count Dracula exclaims, reaching up with both hands.

But before he can pick it up, the gray mist engulfs the Crown of Souls inside a mini cyclone, breaking it into a thousand pieces!

"No!" Count Dracula yells.

"Bram!" comes a familiar voice. "Strike now!"

I look over to find Van Helsing crawling across the floor, and I realize what he's saying.

Count Dracula is distracted.

Despite the pain coursing through my body, I muster all of my willpower and spring up. And then I drive the Eternal Stake straight into Count Dracula's back!

"AAAAAHHHHHHHH!" he screams, his voice echoing through the chamber and inside my brain.

Suddenly, the Eternal Stake gets too hot to hold and I release it just as it turns bright yellow! Smoke pours out of Count Dracula's back as he stumbles to his knees. I step back in horror as Count Dracula looks at me, his eyes wide with surprise. And as he opens his mouth to speak, his fangs gleam, and then his entire body explodes in a blinding flash of yellow light!

I turn away, shielding my eyes, and when I look back, there's nothing left but a black scorch mark on the stone floor.

I drop to my knees and look for any trace of black mist, any trace of Count Dracula's spirit getting away, escaping to fight another day. But… there's nothing.

And… that gray mist? It's gone too.

What was that?

For some reason, I remember the picture inside my hoodie pocket. I reach inside and touch it, but it's deteriorated into pulp. It must have gotten drenched when I was fighting in the swamp.

"Bram," I hear Van Helsing say. "You did it!"

I… did it? I mean, he's right, I just destroyed Count Dracula, once and for all. But instead of feeling elated, I feel… down. And my shoulder hurts so bad.

I touch it again and wince in pain. Suddenly, I don't feel… like myself. In fact, all I feel is hunger. I'm ravenous. I need food. But all I want… is blood.

"Bram," Van Helsing says, blood still trickling down his face. "That is a big wound. How do you feel?"

"N-Not good," I say, my vision hazy. But for some reason, I can't stop looking at the blood dribbling down his chin. It looks so… good.

"Bram?" Van Helsing says.

Suddenly, he's blocked the blood with something, and when my focus comes back I notice he's sitting up, and he's pointing his Crossbow of Purity at me!

"Tell me," Van Helsing says. "Can you feel Count Dracula's venom coursing through your veins?"

"Y-Yeah," I say.

My insides are… burning.

And that's when I realize my worst fears have come

Fifteen

true.

"H-Headmaster," I say.

"Yes, Bram," Van Helsing says, studying me closely.

"I-I think it's too late for me. I-I think you need to... destroy me. At least... my mortal body. Hopefully, I... I won't come back."

"Bram..." he says.

"N-No," I say. "Y-You don't understand. The h-hunger is so strong. This time, I won't be able to c-control it. I-I know you've wanted to... do this for a long time. I... I guess that's why you didn't tell me about the E-Eternal Stake, right?"

"No, Bram," he says. "That is not true."

"I-It doesn't m-matter," I say. "Look, th-thanks for helping me when no one else would. I-I think of you like a father. Always wanted to... please you. B-But I need you to help me now. I-I promised myself I... wouldn't become a full v-vampire. P-Please, destroy me. And tell the t-team I... I'll miss them. Especially Rage... and... and Aura."

Tears stream down my face as I think of their faces.

I'm going to miss them. But I just can't hurt anyone else. It's time.

"P-Please," I repeat. "H-Help me."

"Bram," Van Helsing says. "I am so sorry for what I am about to do."

I see him raise the Crossbow of Purity.

"P-Please..."

THWIP!
I feel something pierce my body.
And then everything goes black.

EPILOGUE

THE AFTERMATH

I hear beeping.

Why is there beeping? I try opening my eyes but my eyelids feel stuck together. After a few failed attempts, I finally manage to pry them open, only to discover I'm lying in a familiar white room with tubes sticking out of my arm.

I'm in the infirmary.

And then I notice I'm not alone.

"How long have I been here?" I ask.

"Three weeks," Van Helsing says, sliding his chair closer to my bed.

"Am I dead?" I ask.

"No," Van Helsing says. "But you were in a coma. Your injury was quite severe. We are very lucky you are alive."

"Yeah, but my body doesn't feel so lucky," I say,

rubbing my eyes. I try sitting up but a dull pain shoots through my right leg. And when I look down my thigh is wrapped in a heavy bandage. "What happened?"

"Please, try to relax," Van Helsing says. "It will take time for you to fully heal. After you destroyed Count Dracula, his venom was rapidly taking over your body, accelerating the multiplication of your own vampiric cells. To stop this infection, I was forced to shoot you in the leg with the Crossbow of Purity."

"Really?" I say, vaguely remembering Van Helsing aiming his weapon at me. "And that worked?"

"Fortunately, yes," he says. "The Crossbow of Purity is a Supernatural artifact that enhances the power of one hundred percent pure silver, the only substance known to purify a vampiric virus. If I did not shoot you immediately, the virus would have taken over and you would have become a full vampire."

"Oh," I say, totally shocked. "But does that mean I'm no longer a vampire?"

"No," Van Helsing says. "Once the crossbow bolt was removed, your DNA took over again. You are still a vampire. Or rather, half-vampire. But you will likely retain some of the purifying effects of the Crossbow of Purity in your bloodstream, which should prevent you from ever becoming a full vampire in the future."

"Really?" I say. Suddenly, it feels like the weight of the world is lifted from my shoulders. I-I can't believe it. I won't ever have to worry about losing control again.

Epilogue

Just being half-vampire never felt so good.

But as I look at Van Helsing, another thought crosses my mind. "You know, I... I thought you were going to kill me."

"Bram," he says, putting his hand on my arm. "I told you I would stand by you from the beginning, and I am a man of my word. Taking your life was never an option."

I look into his determined eyes and wonder why I ever doubted him. But there were so many red flags. So many question marks, like—

"But what about the Eternal Stake?" I say. "Why didn't you tell me about it?"

"I intended to," Van Helsing says, "when the time was right. However, if I told you before you were ready, I feared you would run off with it in pursuit of Count Dracula. After all, you and your friends do have a habit of breaking the rules."

"My friends!" I say, sitting up, the pain returning.

"They are fine," Van Helsing reassures me. "All of them. And they have visited you frequently."

I lie back down relieved. Thank goodness they're okay. If anything happened to them because of me...

Then, I realize Van Helsing is wearing his scarf.

"Headmaster?" I say. "Count Dracula bit you, but somehow you resisted him?"

"Yes," Van Helsing says, removing his jacket and rolling up his sleeve. And that's when I see a bandage covering his entire forearm. "Suspecting his motives before I traveled to New York City, I inserted a sliver of the Crossbow of Purity directly into my arm. His venom never affected me."

"Wow," I say. "That sounds painful but smart. Now that Count Dracula is gone, what happens next?"

"The Dark Ones have crawled back into their holes," Van Helsing says. "Without a leader, I do not think we will be hearing from them anytime soon. But darkness will always try to blot out the light."

I think about what he said and he's right. But now I know I'll always be there to stop them, no matter what.

And speaking of darkness...

"What about Dr. Renfield?" I ask. "What happened to him?"

"I let him go," Van Helsing says.

"He was innocent in all of this, wasn't he?" I say.

"Yes," Van Helsing says. "Dr. Renfield is a good man who was an unwitting victim of Count Dracula, just like you and me. And with Count Dracula gone for good, Dr. Renfield is finally free."

I hope Dr. Renfield is able to move on with his life. What he did wasn't his fault and he deserves a second chance. Then, I see my gray hoodie hanging on the back of the door and it triggers another memory.

"The gray mist!" I say, sitting up again. "Did you see it? I-I didn't tell you about it the first time, but it saved me from DSI. And then it saved me again from Count Dracula. But I... I don't know what it is."

Epilogue

"Are you sure you do not know?" Van Helsing says, with a wry smile. "I suspect you do. But just in case, I have something for you."

Then, he reaches down and hands me a rectangular object wrapped in newspaper. I don't know what it is. I mean, Van Helsing has never given me anything before. And when I unwrap it there is a framed photo of my dad!

It's the same picture that was on his profile!

"That is your father, Gabriel," Van Helsing says. "I found the remnants of his profile in your sweatshirt. As you can imagine, it was not easy to find the original photograph in my office, but I was determined. It was taken the day we admitted him to the academy. He was young and full of energy, just like you."

"So," I say stunned. "A-Are you saying that gray mist... was him?"

"Yes," Van Helsing says. "Since your father was killed by men and not a vampire, his spirit lives on. It is a miracle he has found you again."

"I... I don't know what to say," I respond, my eyes getting watery.

I look out the window at the blue sky. So, that means my father is still out there, watching over me.

Protecting me.

"I know he is proud of you," Van Helsing says. "And so am I."

"That means a lot," I say, wiping my eyes. "You know, it's funny, but with Count Dracula finally gone I'm not sure what I'm supposed to do next."

"Well," Van Helsing says. "I have been thinking about that very topic. I happen to have an opening on my staff for a Survival Skills professor, and I was thinking there is no one more expert in the subject than you."

"Wait, what?" I say.

"You are still a bit young now," Van Helsing says, "But while you continue your studies here at the academy, I would like to invite you to be a Teaching Assistant to Crawler who will fill the role until you are old enough to assume the position on your own. The students would learn a great deal from you, and I know Professor Hexum would be honored to have you as his eventual successor."

"Seriously?" I say.

"Seriously," Van Helsing says. "Professor Hexum may not have always shown it, but he had great respect for your work ethic, character, and courage."

"Wow," I say. "I-I'm honored. But you really want me to be a teacher here?"

"I could not think of anyone more qualified for the job," Van Helsing says. "Unless, of course, you do not want it."

"No!" I say. "I... I would love to. Thank you."

"You are very welcome," Van Helsing says. "And thank you for everything you have done. The entire world is indebted to you. You have saved us all from a most terrible fate."

"Gee, thanks," I say.

Epilogue

"You are a hero," Van Helsing says. "And though we have purged the world of one crisis, there is still much work to do to convince Naturals that monsters are not a threat and we can all live in peace."

"That's for sure," I say, thinking about monster hunters like Agent M. "And you can count on me."

"I know I can," Van Helsing says. "And I will always be here for you."

And then Van Helsing leans in and hugs me.

At first, I'm so shocked I don't know what to do. I mean, I don't remember any adult ever hugging me before. But then I realize how nice it feels and I lean in, hugging him back tightly.

"I am proud of you," Van Helsing says, finally letting go. "Now we should share the good news of your awakening with the others."

Van Helsing stands up, opens the door, and my friends come storming in. Aura, Rage, and the whole gang circle my bed and I can't stop smiling.

"Take it easy on him," Van Helsing says. "He has been through a lot." Then, he winks and leaves.

"Bram," Aura says, "I'm so happy you're okay."

"Thanks," I say, "you have no idea how happy I am to see you guys."

"You really did it," Rage says, slapping the bed railing. "You defeated Count Dracula. I knew you could do it!"

"Well, that makes one of us," I say. "But really, we all did it, together."

"The best part is that it's over," Aura says, smiling at me. "And you can finally get some peace of mind."

"Are you kidding?" InvisiBill says. "The best part is that we'll never have to take Survival Skills again!"

"For sure!" Hairball says, high-fiving Stanphibian.

I smile and decide to keep my mouth shut.

At least for now.

And as I look at my friends gathered around me, and the picture of my father in my hands, I feel happy knowing that for once in my life, I'm finally home.

DON'T MISS EPIC ZERO!

Growing up in a superhero family is cool, unless you're powerless...
Gold Medal Winner - Readers' Favorite Book Awards

Epic Zero: Tales of a Not-So-Super 6th Grader is the first book in a hilarious, action-packed series that will entertain kids, middle school students, and adults!

YOU CAN MAKE A BIG DIFFERENCE

Calling all monsters! I need your help to get Monster Problems 3 in front of more readers.

Reviews are extremely helpful in getting attention for my books. I wish I had the marketing muscle of the major publishers, but instead, I have something far more valuable, loyal readers, just like you! Your generosity in providing an honest review will help bring this book to the attention of more readers.

So, if you've enjoyed this book, I would be very grateful if you could leave a quick review on the book's Amazon page.

Thanks for your support!

R.L. Ullman

ABOUT THE AUTHOR

R.L. Ullman is the bestselling author of the award-winning EPIC ZERO series and the award-winning MONSTER PROBLEMS series. He creates fun, engaging page-turners that captivate the imaginations of kids and adults alike. His original, relatable characters face adventure and adversity that bring out their inner strengths. He's frequently distracted thinking up new stories, and once got lost in his own neighborhood. You can learn more about what R.L. is up to at rlullman.com, and if you see him wandering around your street please point him in the right direction home.

For news, updates, and free stuff, please sign up for the Epic Newsflash at rlullman.com.

***

As always, I would like to thank my Supernatural wife, Lynn, and my freakishly creative kids, Matthew and Olivia, for their undying support.

Made in the USA
Las Vegas, NV
07 December 2020